Mary Eleanor Wilkins Freeman

Silence

And Other Stories

Mary Eleanor Wilkins Freeman

Silence
And Other Stories

ISBN/EAN: 9783337005290

Printed in Europe, USA, Canada, Australia, Japan

Cover: Foto ©Thomas Meinert / pixelio.de

More available books at **www.hansebooks.com**

[Page 38

"'DAVID!' SHE CALLED. 'DAVID! DAVID! DAVID!'"

SILENCE

AND OTHER STORIES

By MARY E. WILKINS

Author of "Jerome, A Poor Man" "Madelon" "Jane Field"

WITH ILLUSTRATIONS

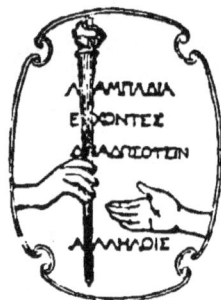

NEW YORK AND LONDON
HARPER & BROTHERS PUBLISHERS
1898

By MARY E. WILKINS.

JEROME, A POOR MAN. A Novel. Illustrated.
Post 8vo, Cloth, $1 50.

MADELON. A Novel. 16mo, Cloth, $1 25.

PEMBROKE. A Novel. Illustrated. 16mo, Cloth,
$1·50.

JANE FIELD. A Novel. Illustrated. 16mo, Cloth,
$1 25.

A HUMBLE ROMANCE, and Other Stories. 16mo,
Cloth, $1 25.

A NEW ENGLAND NUN, and Other Stories. 16mo,
Cloth, $1 25.

YOUNG LUCRETIA, and Other Stories. Illustrated.
Post 8vo, Cloth, $1 25.

GILES COREY, YEOMAN. Illustrated. 32mo, Cloth,
50 cents.

NEW YORK AND LONDON:
HARPER & BROTHERS, PUBLISHERS.

CONTENTS

ILLUSTRATIONS

SILENCE

At dusk Silence went down the Deerfield
street to Ensign John Sheldon's house. She
wore her red blanket over her head, pinned
closely under her chin, and her white profile
showed whiter between the scarlet folds. She
had been spinning all day, and shreds of wool
still clung to her indigo petticoat; now and then
one floated off on the north wind. It was bitter cold, and the snow was four feet deep.
Silence's breath went before her in a cloud; the
snow creaked under her feet. All over the village the crust was so firm that men could walk
upon it. The houses were half sunken in sharp,
rigid drifts of snow; their roofs were laden with
it; icicles hung from the eaves. All the elms
were white with snow frozen to them so strong-
ly that it was not shaken off when they were
lashed by the fierce wind.

There was an odor of boiling meal in the air;
the housewives were preparing supper. Silence
had eaten hers; she and her aunt, Widow Eunice

A 1

Bishop, supped early. She had not far to go to Ensign Sheldon's. She was nearly there when she heard quick footsteps on the creaking snow behind her. Her heart beat quickly, but she did not look around. "Silence," said a voice. Then she paused, and waited, with her eyes cast down and her mouth grave, until David Walcott reached her. "What do you out this cold night, sweetheart?" he said.

"I am going down to Goodwife Sheldon's," replied Silence. Then suddenly she cried out, wildly: "Oh, David, what is that on your cloak? What is it?"

David looked curiously at his cloak. "I see naught on my cloak save old weather stains," said he. "What mean you, Silence?"

Silence quieted down suddenly. "It is gone now," said she, in a subdued voice.

"What did you see, Silence?"

Silence turned towards him; her face quivered convulsively. "I saw a blotch of blood," she cried. "I have been seeing them everywhere all day. I have seen them on the snow as I came along."

David Walcott looked down at her in a bewildered way. He carried his musket over his shoulder, and was shrugged up in his cloak; his heavy, flaxen mustache was stiff and white with frost. He had just been relieved from his post as sentry, and it was no child's play to patrol

2

Deerfield village on a day like that, nor had it been for many previous days. The weather had been so severe that even the French and Indians, lurking like hungry wolves in the neighborhood, had hesitated to descend upon the town, and had stayed in camp.

"What mean you, Silence?" he said.

"What I say," returned Silence, in a strained voice. "I have seen blotches of blood everywhere all day. The enemy will be upon us."

David laughed loudly, and Silence caught his arm. "Don't laugh so loud," she whispered. Then David laughed again. "You be all overwrought, sweetheart," said he. "I have kept guard all the afternoon by the northern palisades, and I have seen not so much as a red fox on the meadow. I tell thee the French and Indians have gone back to Canada. There is no more need of fear."

"I have started all day and all last night at the sound of warwhoops," said Silence.

"Thy head is nigh turned with these troublous times, poor lass. We must cross the road now to Ensign Sheldon's house. Come quickly, or you will perish in this cold."

"Nay, my head is not turned," said Silence, as they hurried on over the crust; "the enemy be hiding in the forests beyond the meadows. David, they be not gone."

"And I tell thee they be gone, sweetheart.

Think you not we should have seen their camp smoke had they been there? And we have had trusty scouts out. Come in, and my aunt, Hannah Sheldon, shall talk thee out of this folly."

The front windows of John Sheldon's house were all flickering red from the hearth fire. David flung open the door, and they entered. There was such a goodly blaze from the great logs in the wide fireplace that even the shadows in the remote corners of the large keeping-room were dusky red, and the faces of all the people in the room had a clear red glow upon them.

Goodwife Hannah Sheldon stood before the fire, stirring some porridge in a great pot that hung on the crane; some fair-haired children sat around a basket shelling corn, a slight young girl in a snuff-yellow gown was spinning, and an old woman in a quilted hood crouched in a corner of the fireplace, holding out her lean hands to the heat.

Goodwife Sheldon turned around when the door opened. "Good-day, Mistress Silence Hoit," she called out, and her voice was sweet, but deep like a man's. "Draw near to the fire, for in truth you must be near perishing with the cold."

"There'll be fire enough ere morning, I trow, to warm the whole township," said the old woman in the corner. Her small black eyes gleamed sharply out of the gloom of her great hood; her

4

yellow face was all drawn and puckered towards the centre of her shrewdly leering mouth.

"Now you hush your croaking, Goody Crane," cried Hannah Sheldon. "Draw the stool near to the fire for Silence, David. I cannot stop stirring, or the porridge will burn. How fares your aunt this cold weather, Silence?"

"Well, except for her rheumatism," replied Silence. She sat down on the stool that David placed for her, and slipped her blanket back from her head. Her beautiful face, full of a grave and delicate stateliness, drooped towards the fire, her smooth fair hair was folded in clear curves like the leaves of a lily around her ears, and she wore a high, transparent, tortoise-shell comb like a coronet in the knot at the back of her head.

David Walcott had pulled off his cap and cloak, and stood looking down at her. "Silence is all overwrought by this talk of Indians," he remarked, presently, and a blush came over his weather-beaten blond face at the tenderness in his own tone.

"The Indians have gone back to Canada," said Goodwife Sheldon, in a magisterial voice. She stirred the porridge faster; it was steaming fiercely.

"So I tell her," said David.

Silence looked up in Hannah Sheldon's sober, masterly face. "Goodwife, may I have a word in private with you?" she asked, in a half-whisper.

5

"As soon as I take the porridge off," replied Goodwife Sheldon.

"God grant it be not the last time she takes the porridge off!" said the old woman.

Hannah Sheldon laughed. "Here be Goody Crane in a sorry mind to-night," said she. "Wait till she have a sup of this good porridge, and I trow she'll pack off the Indians to Canada in a half-hour!"

Hannah began dipping out the porridge. When she had placed generous dishes of it on the table and bidden everybody draw up, she motioned to Silence. "Now, Mistress Silence," said she, "come into the bedroom if you would have a word with me."

Silence followed her into the little north room opening out of the keeping-room, where Ensign John Sheldon and his wife Hannah had slept for many years. It was icy cold, and the thick fur of frost on the little window-panes sent out sparkles in the candle-light. The two women stood beside the great chintz draped and canopied bed, Hannah holding the flaring candle. "Now, what is it?" said she.

"Oh, Goodwife Sheldon!" said Silence. Her face remained quite still, but it was as if one could see her soul fluttering beneath it.

"You be all overwrought, as David saith," cried Goodwife Sheldon, and her voice had a motherly harshness in it. Silence had no mother,

6

and her lover, David Walcott, had none. Hannah
was his aunt, and loved him like her son, so
she felt towards Silence as towards her son's
betrothed.

"In truth I know not what it is," said Silence,
in a kind of reserved terror, " but there has been
all day a great heaviness of spirit upon me, and
last night I dreamed. All day I have fancied
I saw blood here and there. Sometimes, when
I have looked out of the window, the whole snow
hath suddenly glared with red. Goodwife Sheldon, think you the Indians and the French have
in truth gone back to Canada?"

Goodwife Sheldon hesitated a moment, then
she spoke up cheerily. "In truth have they!"
cried she. "John said but this noon that naught
of them had been seen for some time."

"So David said," returned Silence; "but this
heaviness will not be driven away. You know
how Parson Williams hath spoken in warning in
the pulpit and elsewhere, and besought us to
be vigilant. He holdeth that the savages be not
gone."

Hannah Sheldon smiled. "Parson Williams
is a godly man, but prone ever to look upon the
dark side," said she.

"If the Indians should come to-night—" said
Silence.

"I tell ye they will not come, child. I shall
lay me down in that bed a-trusting in the Lord,

7

and having no fear against the time I shall arise from it."

"If the Indians should come— Goodwife Sheldon, be not angered; hear me. If they should come, I pray you keep David here to defend you in this house, and let him not out to seek me. You know well that our house is musket-proof as well as this, and it has long been agreed that they who live nearest, whose houses have not thick walls, shall come to ours and help us make defence. I pray you let not David out of the house to seek me, should there be a surprise to-night. I pray you give me your promise for this, Goodwife Sheldon."

Hannah Sheldon laughed. "In truth will I give thee the promise, if it makes thee easier, child," said she. "At the very first war-screech will I tie David in the chimney-corner with my apron-string, unless you lend me yours. But there will be no war-screech to-night, nor to-morrow night, nor the night after that. The Lord will preserve His people that trust in Him. To-day have I set a web of linen in the loom, and I have candles ready to dip to-morrow, and the day after that I have a quilting. I look not for Indians. If they come I will set them to work. Fear not for David, sweetheart. In truth you should have a bolder heart, an' you look to be a soldier's wife some day."

"I would I had never been aught to him, that

he might not be put in jeopardy to defend me!" said Silence, and her words seemed visible in a white cloud at her mouth.

"We must not stay here in the cold," said Goodwife Sheldon. "Out with ye, Silence, and have a sup of hot porridge, and then David shall see ye home."

Silence sipped a cup of the hot porridge obediently, then she pinned her red blanket over her head. Hannah Sheldon assisted her, bringing it warmly over her face. "'Tis bitter cold," she said. "Now have no more fear, Mistress Silence; the Indians will not come to-night; but do you come over to-morrow, and keep me company while I dip the candles."

"There'll be company enough—there'll be a whole houseful," muttered the old woman in the corner; but nobody heeded her. She was a lonely and wretched old creature whom people sheltered from pity, although she was somewhat feared and held in ill repute. There were rumors that she was well versed in all the dark lore of witchcraft, and held commerce with unlawful beings. The children of Deerfield village looked askance at her, and clung to their mothers if they met her on the street, for they whispered among themselves that old Goody Crane rode through the air on a broom in the night-time.

Silence and David passed out into the keen night. "If you meet my good-man, hasten him home, for the porridge is cooling," Hannah Sheldon called after them.

They met not a soul on Deerfield street, and parted at Silence's door. David would have entered had she bidden him, but she said peremptorily that she had a hard task of spinning that evening, and then she wished him good-night, and without a kiss, for Silence Hoit was chary of caresses. But to-night she called him back ere he was fairly in the street. "David," she called, and he ran back.

"What is it, Silence?" he asked.

She put back her blanket, threw her arms around his neck, and clung to him trembling.

"Why, sweetheart," he whispered, "what has come over thee?"

"You know—this house is made like—a fort," she said, bringing out her words in gasps, "and —there are muskets, and — powder stored in it, and—Captain Moulton, and his sons, and—John Carson will come, and make—a stand in it. I have—no fear should—the Indians come. Remember that I have no fear, and shall be safe here, David."

David laughed, and patted her clinging shoulders. "Yes, I will remember, Silence," he said; "but the Indians will not come."

"Remember that I am safe here, and have no fear," she repeated. Then she kissed him of her own accord, as if she had been his wife, and

10

entered the house, and he went away, wondering.

Silence's aunt, Widow Eunice Bishop, did not look up when the door opened; she was knitting by the fire, sitting erect with her mouth pursed. She had a hostile expression, as if she were listening to some opposite argument. Silence hung her blanket on a peg; she stood irresolute a minute, then she breathed on the frosty window and cleared a space through which she could look out. Her aunt gave a quick, fierce glance at her, then she tossed back her head and knitted. Silence stood staring out of the little peep-hole in the frosty pane. Her aunt glanced at her again, then she spoke.

"I should think if you had been out gossiping and gadding for two hours, you had better get yourself at some work now," she said, "unless your heart be set on idling. A pretty housewife you'll make!"

"Come here quick, quick!" Silence cried out.

Her aunt started, but she would not get up; she knitted, scowling. "I cannot afford to idle if other folk can," said she. "I have no desire to keep running to windows and standing there gaping, as you have done all this day."

"Oh, aunt, I pray you to come," said Silence, and she turned her white face over her shoulder towards her aunt; "there is somewhat wrong surely."

Widow Bishop got up, still scowling, and went over to the window. Silence stood aside and pointed to the little clear circle in the midst of the frost. "Over there to the north," she said, in a quick, low voice.

Her aunt adjusted her horn spectacles and bent her head stiffly. "I see naught," said she.

"A red glare in the north!"

"A red glare in the north! Be ye out of your mind, wench! There be no red glare in the north. Everything be quiet in the town. Get ye away from the window and to your work. I have no more patience with such doings. Here have I left my knitting for nothing, and I just about setting the heel. You'd best keep to your spinning instead of spying out of the window at your own nightmares, and gadding about the town after David Walcott. Pretty doings for a modest maid, I call it, following after young men in this fashion!"

Silence turned on her aunt, and her blue eyes gleamed dark; she held up her head like a queen. "I follow not after young men," she said.

"Heard I not David Walcott's voice at the door? Went you not to Goodwife Sheldon's, where he lives? Was it not his voice—hey?"

"Yes, 'twas, an' I had a right to go there an I chose, an' 'twas naught unmaidenly," said Silence.

"'Twas unmaidenly in my day," retorted her

12

aunt; "perhaps 'tis different now." She had returned to her seat, and was clashing her knitting-needles like two swords in a duel.

Silence pulled a spinning-wheel before the fire and fell to work. The wheel turned so rapidly that the spokes were a revolving shadow; there was a sound as if a bee had entered the room.

"I stayed at home, and your uncle did the courting," Widow Eunice Bishop continued, in a voice that demanded response.

But Silence made none. She went on spinning. Her aunt eyed her maliciously. "I never went after nightfall to his house that he might see me home," said she. "I trow my mother would have locked me up in the garret, and kept me on meal and water for a week, had I done aught so bold."

Silence spun on. Her aunt threw her head back, and knitted, jerking out her elbows. Neither of them spoke again until the clock struck nine. Then Widow Bishop wound her ball of yarn closer, and stuck in the knitting-needles, and rose. "'Tis time to put out the candle," she said, "and *I* have done a good day's work, and feel need of rest. They that have idled cannot make it up by wasting tallow." She threw open the door that led to her bedroom, and a blast of icy confined air rushed in. She untied the black cap that framed her nervous

face austerely, and her gray head, with its tight
rosette of hair on the crown, appeared. Silence
set her spinning-wheel back, and raked the ashes
over the hearth fire. Then she took the candle
and climbed the stairs to her own chamber. Her
aunt was already in bed, her pale, white-frilled
face sunk in the icy feather pillow; but she did
not bid her good-night: not on account of her
anger; there was seldom any such formal courtesy exchanged between the women. Silence's
chamber had one side sloping with the slope of
the roof, and in it were two dormer-windows
looking towards the north. She set her candle
on the table, breathed on one of these windows,
as she had on the one down-stairs, and looked
out. She stood there several minutes, then she
turned away, shaking her head. The room was
very cold. She let down her smooth fair hair,
and her fingers began to redden; she took off
her kerchief; then she stopped, and looked hesitatingly at her bed, with its blue curtains. She
set her mouth hard, and put on her kerchief.
Then she sat down on the edge of her bed and
waited. After a while she pulled a quilt from
the bed and wrapped it around her. Still she did
not shiver. She had blown out the candle, and
the room was very dark. All her nerves seemed
screwed tight like fiddle-strings, and her thoughts
beat upon them and made terrific waves of sound
in her ears. She saw sparks and flashes like dia-

mond fire in the darkness. She had her hands
clinched tight, but she did not feel her hands nor
her feet—she did not feel her whole body. She
sat so until two o'clock in the morning. When
the clock down in the keeping-room struck the
hours, the peals shocked her back for a minute
to her old sense of herself; then she lost it again.
Just after the clock struck two, while the silvery
reverberation of the bell tone was still in her ears,
and she was breathing a little freer, a great rosy
glow suffused the frosty windows. A horrible
discord of sound arose without. Above everything else came something like a peal of laughter
from wild beasts or fiends.

Silence arose and went down-stairs. Her aunt
rushed out of her bedroom, shrieking, and caught
hold of her. "Oh, Silence, what is it, what is
it?" she cried.

"Get away till I light a candle," said Silence.
She fairly pushed her aunt off, shovelled the
ashes from the coals in the fireplace, and lighted
a candle. Then she threw some wood on the
smouldering fire. Her aunt was running around
the room screaming. There came a great pound
on the door.

"It's the Indians! it's the Indians! don't let
'em in!" shrieked her aunt. "Don't let them
in! don't let them!" She placed her lean
shoulder in her white bed-gown against the
door. "Go away! go away!" she yelled.

"You can't come in! O Lord Almighty, save us!"

"You stand off," said Silence. She took hold of her aunt's shoulders. "Be quiet," she commanded. Then she called out, in a firm voice, "Who is there?"

At the shout in response she drew the great iron bolts quickly and flung open the heavy nail-studded door. There was a press of frantic, white-faced people into the room; then the door was slammed to and the bolts shot. It was very still in the room, except for the shuffling rush of the men's feet, and now and then a stern, gasping order. The children did not cry; all the noise was without. The house might have stood in the midst of some awful wilderness peopled with fiendish beasts, from the noise without. The cries seemed actually in the room. The children's eyes glared white over their mothers' shoulders.

The men hurriedly strengthened the window-shutters with props of logs, and fitted the muskets into the loop-holes. Suddenly there was a great crash at the door, and a wilder yell outside. The muskets opened fire, and some of the women rushed to the door and pressed fiercely against it with their delicate shoulders, their white, desperate faces turning back dumbly, like a spiritual phalanx of defence. Silence and her aunt were among them.

Suddenly Widow Eunice Bishop, at a fresh onslaught upon the door, and a fiercer yell, lifted up her voice and shrieked back in a rage as mad as theirs. Her speech, too, was almost inarticulate, and the sense of it lost in a savage frenzy; her tongue stuttered over abusive epithets; but for a second she prevailed over the terrible chorus without. It was like the solo of a fury. Then louder yells drowned her out; the muskets cracked faster; the men rammed in the charges; the savages fell back somewhat; the blows on the door ceased.

Silence ran up the stairs to her chamber, and peeped cautiously out of a little dormer-window. Deerfield village was roaring with flames, the sky and snow were red, and leaping through the glare came the painted savages, a savage white face and the waving sword of a French officer in their midst. The awful warwhoops and the death-cries of her friends and neighbors sounded in her ears. She saw, close under her window, the dark sweep of the tomahawk, the quick glance of the scalping-knife, and the red starting of caps of blood. She saw infants dashed through the air, and the backward-straining forms of shrieking women dragged down the street; but she saw not David Walcott anywhere.

She eyed in an agony some dark bodies lying like logs in the snow. A wild impulse seized her to run out, turn their dead faces, and see that none of them was her lover's. Her room was full of red light; everything in it showed distinctly. The roof of the next house crashed in, and the sparks and cinders shot up like a volcano. There was a great outcry of terror from below, and Silence hurried down. The Indians were trying to fire the house from the west side. They had piled a bank of brush against it, and the men had hacked new loop-holes and were beating them back.

John Carson's wife clutched Silence as she entered the keeping-room. "They are trying to set the house on fire," she gasped, "and — the bullets are giving out!" The woman held a little child hugged close to her breast; she strained him closer. "They shall not have him, anyway," she said. Her mouth looked white and stiff.

"Put him down and help, then," said Silence. She began pulling the pewter plates off the dresser.

"What be you doing with my pewter plates?" screamed her aunt at her elbow.

Silence said nothing. She went on piling the plates under her arm.

"Think you I will have the pewter plates I have had ever since I was wed, melted to make bullets for those limbs of Satan?"

Silence carried the plates to the fire; the women piled on wood and made it hotter. John Carson's wife laid her baby on the settle and helped, and Widow Bishop brought out her pew-

ter spoons, and her silver cream-jug when the
pewter ran low, and finally her dead husband's
knee-buckles from the cedar chest. All the pewter and silver in Widow Eunice Bishop's house
were melted down that night. The women worked
with desperate zeal to supply the men with bullets, and just before the ammunition failed, the
Indians left Deerfield village, with their captives
in their train.

The men had stopped firing at last. Everything was quiet outside, except for the flurry of
musket-shots down on the meadow, where the
skirmish was going on between the Hatfield men
and the retreating French and Indians. The
dawn was breaking, but not a shutter had been
stirred in the Bishop house; the inmates were
clustered together, their ears straining for another
outburst of slaughter.

Suddenly there was a strange crackling sound
overhead; a puff of hot smoke came into the
room from the stairway. The roof had caught
fire from the shower of sparks, and the stanch
house that had withstood all the fury of the savages was going the way of its neighbors.

The men rushed up the stair, and fell back.
"We can't save it!" Captain Isaac Moulton said,
hoarsely. He was an old man, and his white hair
tossed wildly around his powder-blackened face.

Widow Eunice Bishop scuttled into her bedroom, and got her best silk hood and her gilt-

framed looking-glass. "Silence, get out the feather-bed!" she shrieked.

The keeping-room was stifling with smoke. Captain Moulton loosened a window-shutter cautiously and peered out. "I see no sign of the savages," he said. They unbolted the door, and opened it inch by inch, but there was no exultant shout in response. The crack of muskets on the meadow sounded louder; that was all.

Widow Eunice Bishop pushed forward before the others; the danger by fire to her household goods had driven her own danger from her mind, which could compass but one terror at a time. "Let me forth!" she cried; and she laid the looking-glass and silk hood on the snow, and pelted back into the smoke for her feather-bed and the best andirons.

Silence carried out the spinning-wheel, and the others caught up various articles which they had wit to see in the panic. They piled them up on the snow outside, and huddled together, staring fearfully down the village street. They saw, amid the smouldering ruins, Ensign John Sheldon's house standing.

"We must make for that," said Captain Isaac Moulton, and they started. The men went before and behind, with their muskets in readiness, and the women and children walked between. Widow Bishop carried the looking-glass; somebody had helped her to bring out her feather-bed, and she had dragged it to a clean place well away from the burning house.

The dawnlight lay pale and cold in the east; it was steadily overcoming the fire-glow from the ruins. Nobody would have known Deerfield village. The night before the sun had gone down upon the snowy slants of humble roofs and the peaceful rise of smoke from pleasant hearth fires. The curtained windows had gleamed out one by one with mild candle-light, and serene faces of white-capped matrons preparing supper had passed them. Now, on both sides of Deerfield street were beds of glowing red coals; grotesque ruins of door-posts and chimneys in the semblances of blackened martyrs stood crumbling in the midst of them, and twisted charred heaps, which the people eyed trembling, lay in the old doorways. The snow showed great red patches in the gathering light, and in them lay still bodies that seemed to move.

Silence Hoit sprang out from the hurrying throng, and turned the head of one dead man whose face she could not see. The horror of his red crown did not move her. She only saw that he was not David Walcott. She stooped and wiped off her hands in some snow.

"That is Israel Bennett," the others groaned.

John Carson's wife had been the dead man's sister. She hugged her baby tighter, and pressed more closely to her husband's back. There was no longer any sound of musketry on the meadows. There was not a sound to be heard except the wind in the dry trees and the panting breaths of the knot of people.

A dead baby lay directly in the path, and a woman caught it up, and tried to warm it at her breast. She wrapped her cloak around it, and wiped its little bloody face with her apron. " 'Tis not dead," she declared, frantically; " the child is not dead !" She had not shed a tear nor uttered a wail before, but now she began sobbing aloud over the dead child. It was Goodwife Barnard's, and no kin to her; she was a single woman. The others were looking right and left for lurking savages; she looked only at the little cold face on her bosom. " The child breathes," she said, and hurried on faster that she might get succor for it.

The party halted before Ensign John Sheldon's house. The stout door was fast, but there was a hole in it, as if hacked by a tomahawk. The men tried it and shook it. " Open, open, Goodwife Sheldon !" they hallooed. " Friends ! friends ! Open the door !" But there was no response.

Silence Hoit left the throng at the door, and began clambering up on a slant of icy snow to a window which was flung wide open. The window-sill was stained with blood, and so was the snow.

One of the men caught Silence and tried to hold her back. "There may be Indians in there," he whispered, hoarsely.

But Silence broke away from him, and was in through the window, and the men followed her, and unbolted the door for the women, who pressed in wildly, and flung it to again. A child who was among them, little Comfort Arms, stationed herself directly with her tiny back against the door, with her mouth set like a soldier's, and her blue eyes gleaming fierce under her flaxen locks. "They shall not get in," said she. Somehow she had gotten hold of a great horse-pistol, which she carried like a doll.

Nobody heeded her, Silence least of all. She stared about the room, with her lips parted. Right before her on the hearth lay a little three-year-old girl, Mercy Sheldon, her pretty head in a pool of blood, but Silence cast only an indifferent glance when the others gathered about her, groaning and sighing.

Suddenly Silence sprang towards a dark heap near the pantry door, but it was only a woman's quilted petticoat.

The spinning-wheel lay broken on the floor, and all the simple furniture was strewn about wildly. Silence went into Goodwife Sheldon's bedroom, and the others followed her, trembling, all except little Comfort Arms, who stood un-flinchingly with her back pressed against the

23

door, and the single woman, Grace Mather; she stayed behind, and put wood on the fire, after she had picked up the quilted petticoat, and laid the dead baby tenderly wrapped in it on the settle. Then she pulled the settle forward before the fire, and knelt before it, and fell to chafing the little limbs of the dead baby, weeping as she did so.

Goodwife Sheldon's bedroom was in wild disorder. A candle still burned, although it was very low, on the table, whose linen cover had great red finger-prints on it. Goodwife Sheldon's decent clothes were tossed about on the floor; the curtains of the bed were half torn away. Silence pressed forward unshrinkingly towards the bed; the others, even the men, hung back. There lay Goodwife Sheldon dead in her bed. All the light in the room, the candle-light and the low daylight, seemed to focus upon her white, frozen profile propped stiffly on the pillow, where she had fallen back when the bullet came through that hole in the door.

Silence looked at her. "Where is David, Goodwife Sheldon?" said she.

Eunice Bishop sprang forward. "Be you clean out of your mind, Silence Hoit?" she cried. "Know you not she's dead? She's dead! Oh, she's dead, she's dead! An' here's her best silk hood trampled underfoot on the floor!" Eunice snatched up the hood, and seized Silence by the arm, but she pushed her back.

"Where is David? Where is he gone?" she demanded again of the dead woman.

The other women came crowding around Silence then, and tried to soothe her and reason with her, while their own faces were white with horror and woe. Goodwife Sarah Spear, an old woman whose sons lay dead in the street outside, put an arm around the girl, and tried to draw her head to her broad bosom.

"Mayhap you will find him, sweetheart," she said. "He's not among the dead out there."

But Silence broke away from the motherly arm, and sped wildly through the other rooms, with the people at her heels, and her aunt crying vainly after her. They found no more dead in the house; naught but ruin and disorder, and bloody footprints and handprints of savages.

When they returned to the keeping-room, Silence seated herself on a stool by the fire, and held out her hands towards the blaze to warm them. The daylight was broad outside now, and the great clock that had come from overseas ticked; the Indians had not touched that.

Captain Isaac Moulton lifted little Mercy Sheldon from the hearth and carried her to her dead mother in the bedroom, and two of the older women went in there and shut the door. Little Comfort Arms still stood with her back against the outer door, and Grace Mather tended the dead baby on the settle.

"What do ye with that dead child?" a woman called out roughly to her.

"I tell ye 'tis not dead; it breathes," returned Grace Mather; and she never turned her harsh, plain face from the dead child.

"An' I tell ye 'tis dead."

"An' I tell ye 'tis not dead. I need but some hot posset for it."

Goodwife Carson began to weep. She hugged her own living baby tighter. "Let her alone!" she sobbed. "I wonder our wits be not all gone." She went sobbing over to little Comfort Arms at the door. "Come away, sweetheart, and draw near the fire," she pleaded, brokenly.

The little girl looked obstinately up at her. "They shall not come in," she said. "The wicked savages shall not come in again."

"No more shall they, an' the Lord be willing, sweet. But, I pray you, come away from the door now."

Comfort shook her head, and she looked like her father as he fought on the Deerfield meadows.

"The savages are gone, sweet."

But Comfort answered not a word, and Goodwife Carson sat down and began to nurse her baby. One of the women hung the porridge-kettle over the fire; another put some potatoes in the ashes to bake. Presently the two women came out of Goodwife Sheldon's bedroom with grave, strained faces, and held their stiff blue fingers out to the hearth fire.

Eunice Bishop, who was stirring the porridge, looked at them with sharp curiosity. "How look they ?" she whispered.

"As peaceful as if they slept," replied Goodwife Spear, who was one of the women.

"And the child's head ?"

"We put on her little white cap with the lace frills."

Eunice stirred the bubbling porridge, scowling in the heat and steam ; some of the women laid the table with Hannah Sheldon's linen cloth and pewter dishes, and presently the breakfast was dished up.

Little Comfort Arms had sunk at the foot of the nail-studded door in a deep slumber. She slept at her post like the faithless sentry whose slumbers the night before had brought about the destruction of Deerfield village. Goodwife Spear raised her up, but her curly head drooped helplessly.

"Wake up, Comfort, and have a sup of hot porridge," she called in her ear.

She led her over to the table, Comfort stumbling weakly at arm's-length, and set her on a stool with a dish of porridge before her, which she ate uncertainly in a dazed fashion, with her eyes filming and her head nodding.

They all gathered gravely around the table,

except Silence Hoit and Grace Mather. Silence sat still, staring at the fire, and Grace had dipped out a little cup of the hot porridge, and was trying to feed it to the dead baby, with crooning words.

"Silence, why come you not to the table?" her aunt called out.

"I want nothing," answered Silence.

"I see not why you should so set yourself up before the others, as having so much more to bear," said Eunice, sharply. "There is Goodwife Spear, with her sons unburied on the road yonder, and she eats her porridge with good relish."

John Carson's wife set her baby on her husband's knee, and carried a dish of porridge to Silence.

"Try and eat it, sweet," she whispered. She was near Silence's age.

Silence looked up at her. "I want it not," said she.

"But he may not be dead, sweet. He may presently be home. You would not he should find you spent and fainting. Perchance he may have wounds for you to tend."

Silence seized the dish and began to eat the porridge in great spoonfuls, gulping it down fast.

The people at the table eyed her sadly and whispered, and they also cast frequent glances at Grace Mather bending over the dead baby. Once

Captain Isaac Moulton called out to her in his gruff old voice, which he tried to soften, and she answered back, sharply: "Think ye I will leave this child while it breathes, Captain Isaac Moulton? In faith I am the only one of ye all who has regard to it."

But suddenly, when the meal was half over, Grace Mather arose, and gathered up the little dead baby, carried it into Goodwife Sheldon's bedroom, and was gone some time.

"She has lost her wits," said Eunice Bishop. "Think you not we should follow her? She may do some harm."

"Nay, let her be," said Goodwife Spear.

When at last Grace Mather came out of the bedroom, and they all turned to look at her, her face was stern but quite composed. "I found a little clean linen shift in the chest," she said to Goodwife Spear, who nodded gravely. Then she sat down at the table and ate.

The people, as they ate, cast frequent glances at the barred door and the shuttered windows. The daylight was broad outside, but there was no glimmer of it in the room, and the candles were lighted. They dared not yet remove the barricades, and the muskets were in readiness: the Indians might return.

All at once there was a shrill clamor at the door, and men sprang to their muskets. The women clutched each other, panting.

"Unbar the door!" shrieked a quavering old voice. "I tell ye, unbar the door! I be nigh frozen a-standing here. Unbar the door! The Indians are gone hours ago."

"'Tis Goody Crane!" cried Eunice Bishop.

Captain Isaac Moulton shot back the bolts and opened the door a little way, while the men stood close at his back, and Goody Crane slid in like a swift black shadow out of the daylight.

She crouched down close to the fire, trembling and groaning, and the women gave her some hot porridge.

"Where have ye been?" demanded Eunice Bishop.

"Where they found me not," replied the old woman, and there was a sudden leer like a light in the gloom of her great hood. She motioned towards the bedroom door.

"Goody Sheldon sleeps late this morning, and so doth Mercy," said she. "I trow she will not dip her candles to-day."

The people looked at each other; a subtler horror than that of the night before shook their spirits.

Captain Isaac Moulton towered over the old woman on the hearth. "How knew you Goodwife Sheldon and Mercy were dead?" he asked, sternly.

The old woman leered up at him undauntedly; her head bobbed. There was a curious grotesque-

AT ENSIGN SHELDON'S HOUSE THE MORNING AFTER THE MASSACRE

ness about her blanketed and hooded figure when in motion. There was so little of the old woman herself visible that motion surprised, as it would have done in a puppet. "Told I not Goody Sheldon last night she would never stir porridge again?" said she. "Who stirred the porridge this morning? I trow Goody Sheldon's hands be too stiff and too cold, though they have stirred well in their day. Hath she dipped her candles yet? Hath she begun on her weaving? I trow 'twill be a long day ere Mary Sheldon's linen-chest be filled, if she herself go a-gadding to Canada and her mother sleep so late."

"Eat this hot porridge and stop your croaking," said Goodwife Spear, stooping over her.

The old woman extended her two shaking hands for the dish. "That was what she said last night," she returned. "The living echo the dead, and that is enough wisdom for a witch."

"You'll be burned for a witch yet, Goody Crane, an you be not careful," cried Eunice Bishop.

"There is fire enough outside to burn all the witches in the land," muttered the old woman, sipping her porridge. Suddenly she eyed Silence sitting motionless opposite. "Where be your sweetheart this fine morning, Silence Hoit?" she inquired.

Silence looked at her. There was a strange

likeness between the glitter in her blue eyes and that in Goody Crane's black ones.

The old woman's great hood nodded over the porridge-dish. "I can tell ye, Mistress Silence," she said, thickly, as she ate. "He is gone to Canada on a moose - hunt, and unless I be far wrong, he hath taken thy wits with him."

"How know you David Walcott is gone to Canada?" cried Eunice Bishop; and Silence stared at her with her hard blue eyes.

Silence's soft fair hair hung all matted like uncombed flax over her pale cheeks. There was a rigid, dead look about her girlish forehead and her sweet mouth.

"I know," returned Goody Crane, nodding her head.

The women washed the pewter dishes, set them back on the dresser, and swept the floor. Little Comfort Arms had been carried up-stairs and laid in the bed whence poor Mary Sheldon had been dragged and haled to Canada. The men stood talking near their stacked muskets. One of the shutters had been opened and the candles put out. The winter sun shone in the window as it had shone before, but the poor folk in Ensign Sheldon's keeping-room saw it with a certain shock, as if it were a stranger. That morning their own hearts had in them such strangeness that they transferred it like motion to all familiar objects. The very iron dogs in the Sheldon

32

fireplace seemed on the leap with tragedy, and the porridge-kettle swung darkly out of some former age.

Now and then one of the men opened the door cautiously and peered out and listened. The reek of the smouldering village came in at the door, but there was not a sound except the whistling howl of the savage north wind, which still swept over the valley. There was not a shot to be heard from the meadows. The men discussed the wisdom of leaving the women for a short space and going forth to explore, but Widow Eunice Bishop interposed, thrusting her sharp face in among them.

"Here we be," scolded she, "a passel of women and children, and Hannah Sheldon and Mercy a-lying dead, and me with my house burnt down, and nothing saved except my silk hood and my looking-glass and my feather-bed, and it's a mercy if that's not all smooched, and you talk of going off and leaving us!"

The men looked doubtfully at one another; then there was the hissing creak of footsteps on the snow outside, and Widow Bishop screamed. "Oh, the Indians have come back!" she proclaimed.

Silence looked up.

The door was tried from without.

"Who's there?" cried out Captain Moulton.

"John Sheldon," responded a hoarse voice.
"Who's inside?"

Captain Moulton threw open the door, and
John Sheldon stood there. His severe and sober
face was painted like an Indian's with blood and
powder grime; he stood staring in at the company.

"Come in, quick, and let us bar the door!"
screamed Eunice Bishop.

John Sheldon came in hesitatingly, and stood
looking around the room.

"Have you but just come from the meadows?" inquired Captain Moulton. But John
Sheldon did not seem to hear him. He stared
at the company, who all stood still staring back
at him; then he looked hard and long at the
doors, as if expecting some one to enter. The
eyes of the others followed his, but no one spoke.

"Where's Hannah?" asked John Sheldon.

Then the women began to weep.

"She's in there," sobbed John Carson's wife,
pointing to the bedroom door—"in there with
little Mercy, Goodman Sheldon."

"Is—the child hurt, and—Hannah a-tending
her?"

The women wept, and pushed each other forward to tell him, but Captain Isaac Moulton
spoke out, and drove the knife home like an
honest soldier, who will kill if he must, but not
mangle.

34

"Goodwife Sheldon lies yonder, shot dead in her bed, and we found the child dead on the hearth-stone," said Isaac Moulton.

John Sheldon turned his gaze on him.

"The judgments of the Lord are just and righteous altogether," said Isaac Moulton, confronting him with stern defiance.

"Amen," returned John Sheldon. He took off his cloak, and hung it up on the peg as he was used.

"Where is David Walcott?" asked Silence, standing before him.

"David, he is gone with the Indians to Canada, and the boys, Ebenezer and Remembrance."

"Where is David?"

"I tell ye, lass, he is gone with the French and Indians to Canada; and you need be thankful he was but your sweetheart, and ye not wed, with a half-score of babes to be taken too. The curse that was upon the women of Jerusalem is upon the women of Deerfield." John Sheldon looked sternly into Silence's white wild face; then his voice softened. "Take heart, lass," said he. "Erelong I shall go to Governor Dudley and get help, and then after them to Canada, and fetch them back. Take heart; I will fetch thee thy sweetheart presently."

Silence returned to her seat in the fireplace. Goody Crane looked across at her. "He will come back over the north meadow," she whis-

35

pered. "Keep watch over the north meadow; but 'twill be a long day ere ye see him."

Silence paid seemingly little heed. She paid little heed to Ensign John Sheldon relating how the French and Indians, with Hertel de Rouville at their head, were on the road to Canada with their captives; of the fight on the meadow between the retreating foe and the brave band of Deerfield and Hatfield men, who had made a stand there to intercept them; how they had been obliged to cease firing because the captives were threatened; and the pitiful tale of Parson John Williams, two of whose children were killed, dragged through the wilderness with the others, and his sick wife.

"Had folk listened to him, we had all been safe in our good houses with our belongings," cried Eunice Bishop.

"They will not drag Goodwife Williams far," said Goody Crane, "nor the babe at her breast. I trow well it hath stopped wailing ere now."

"How know you that?" questioned Eunice Bishop, turning sharply on her.

But the old woman only nodded her head, and Silence paid no heed, for she was not there. Her slender girlish shape sat by the hearth fire in John Sheldon's house in Deerfield, her fair head showed like a delicate flower, but Silence Hoit was following her lover to Canada. Every step that he took painfully through pathless forests, on treacherous ice, and desolate snow fields, she took more painfully still; every knife gleaming over his head she saw. She bore his every qualm of hunger and pain and cold, and it was all the harder because they struck on her bare heart with no flesh between, for she sat in the flesh in Deerfield, and her heart went with her lover to Canada.

The sun stood higher, but it was still bitter cold; the blue frost on the windows did not melt, and the icicles on the eaves, which nearly touched the sharp snow-drifts underneath, did not drip. The desolate survivors of the terrible night began work among the black ruins of their homes. They cared as well as they might for the dead in Deerfield street, and the dead on the meadow where the fight had been. Their muscles were all tense with the cold, their faces seamed and blue with it, but their hearts were strained with a fiercer cold than that. Not one man of them but had one or more slain, with dead face upturned, seeking his in the morning light, or on that awful road to Canada. Ever as the men worked they turned their eyes northward, and met grimly the icy blast of the north wind, and sometimes to their excited fancies it seemed to bring to their ears the cries of their friends who were facing it also, and they stood still and listened.

Silence Hoit crept out of the house and down

the road a little way, and then stood looking
over the meadow towards the north. Her fair
hair tossed in the wind, her pale cheeks turned
pink, the wind struck full upon her delicate
figure. She had come out without her blanket.

"David!" she called. "David! David!
David!" The north wind bore down upon her,
shrieking with a wild fury like a savage of the
air; the dry branches of a small tree near her
struck her in the face. "David!" she called
again. "David! David!" She swelled out
her white throat like a bird, and her voice was
shrill and sweet and far-reaching. The men
moving about on the meadow below, and stooping over the dead, looked up at her, but she did
not heed them. She had come through a break
in the palisades; on each side of her the frozen
snow-drifts slanted sharply to their tops, and
they glittered with blue lights like glaciers in
the morning sun over those drifts the enemy had
passed the night before.

The men on the meadow saw Silence's hair
blowing like a yellow banner between the drifts
of snow.

"The poor lass has come out bareheaded,"
said Ensign Sheldon. "She is near out of her
mind for David Walcott."

"A man should have no sweetheart in these
times, unless he would her heart be broke," said
a young man beside him. He was hardly more

than a boy, and his face was as rosy as a girl's in the wind. He kept close to Ensign Sheldon, and his mind was full of young Mary Sheldon travelling to Canada on her weary little feet. He had often, on a Sabbath day, looked across the meeting-house at her, and thought that there was no maiden like her in Deerfield.

Ensign John Sheldon thought of his sweetheart lying with her heart still in her freezing bedroom, and stooped over a dead Hatfield man whose face was frozen into the snow.

The young man, whose name was Freedom Wells, bent over to help him. Then he started. "What's that?" he cried.

" 'Tis only Silence Hoit calling David Walcott again," replied Ensign Sheldon.

The voice had sounded like Mary Sheldon's to Freedom. The tears rolled over his boyish cheeks as he put his hands into the snow and tried to dig it away from the dead man's face.

"David! David! David!" called Silence.

Suddenly her aunt threw a wiry arm around her. "Be you gone clean daft," she shrieked against the wind, "standing here calling David Walcott? Know you not he is a half-day's journey towards Canada an the savages have not scalped him and left him by the way? Standing here with your hair blowing and no blanket! Into the house with ye!"

Silence followed her aunt unresistingly. The

women in Ensign Sheldon's house were hard at
work. They were baking in the great brick
oven, spinning, and even dipping poor Goodwife
Sheldon's candles.

"Bind up your hair, like an honest maid, and
go to spinning," said Eunice, and she pointed to
the spinning-wheel which had been saved from
her own house. "We that be spared have to
work, and not sit down and trot our own hearts
on our knees. There is scarce a yard of linen
left in Deerfield, to say naught of woollen cloth.
Bind up your hair!"

And Silence bound up her hair, and sat down
by her wheel meekly, and yet with a certain dignity. Indeed, through all the disorder of her
mind, that delicate maiden dignity never for-
sook her, and there was never aught but respect
shown her.

As time went on, it became quite evident that
although the fair semblance of Silence Hoit still
walked the Deerfield street, sat in the meeting-
house, and toiled at the spinning-wheel and
the loom, yet she was as surely not there as
though she had been haled to Canada with the
other captives on that terrible February night.
It became the general opinion that Silence Hoit
would never be quite her old self again and
walk in the goodly company of all her fair wits
unless David Walcott should be redeemed from
captivity and restored to her. Then, it was ac-

counted possible, the mending of the calamity which had brought her disorder upon her might remove it.

"Ye wait," Widow Eunice Bishop would say, hetchelling flax the while as though it were the scalp-locks of the enemy—"ye wait. If once David Walcott show his face, ye'll see Silence Hoit be not so lacking. She hath a tenderer heart than some I could mention, who go about smiling when their nearest of kin lay in torment in Indian lodges. She cares naught for picking up a new sweetheart. She hath a steady heart that be not so easy turned as some. Silence was never a light hussy, a-dancing hither and thither off the bridle-path for a new flower on the bushes. An', for all ye call her lacking now, there be not a maid in Deerfield does such a day's task as she."

And that last statement was quite true. All the Deerfield women, the matrons and maidens, toiled unceasingly, with a kind of stern patience like that which served their husbands and lovers in the frontier corn-fields, and which served all the dauntless border settlers, who were forced continually to rebuild after destruction, like way-side ants whose nests are always being trampled underfoot. There was need of unflinching toil at wheel and loom, for there was great scarcity of household linen in Deerfield, and Silence Hoit's shapely white maiden hands flinched less than any.

Nevertheless, many a day, in the morning when the snowy meadows were full of blue lights, at sunset when all the snow levels were rosy, but more particularly in wintry moonlight when the country was like a waste of silver, would Silence Hoit leave suddenly her household task, and hasten to the terrace overlooking the north meadow, and shriek out: " David! David! David Walcott!"

The village children never jeered at her, as they would sometimes jeer at Goody Crane if not restrained by their elders. They eyed with a mixture of wonder and admiration Silence's beautiful bewildered face, with the curves of gold hair around the pink cheeks, and the fretwork of tortoise-shell surmounting it. David Walcott had given Silence her shell comb, and she was never seen without it.

Many a time when Silence called to David from the terrace of the north meadow, some of the little village maids in their homespun pinafores would join her and call with her. They had no fear of her, as they had of Goody Crane.

Indeed, Goody Crane, after the massacre, was in worse repute than ever in Deerfield. There were dark rumors concerning her whereabouts upon that awful night. Some among the devout and godly were fain to believe that the old woman had been in league with the powers of darkness and their allies the savages, and had so escaped harm. Some even whispered that in the thickest of the slaughter, when Deerfield was in the midst of that storm of fire, old Goody Crane's laugh had been heard, and one, looking up, had spied her high overhead riding her broomstick, her face red with the glare of the flames. The old woman was sheltered under protest, and had Deerfield not been a frontier town, and graver matters continually in mind, she might have come to harm in consequence of the gloomy suspicions concerning her.

Many a night after the massacre would the windows fly up and anxious faces peer out. It was as if the ears of the people were tuned up to the pitch of the Indian warwhoops, and their very thoughts made the nights ring with them.

The palisades were well looked to; there was never a slope of frozen snow again to form foothold for the enemy, and the sentry never slept at his post. But the anxious women listened all winter for the warwhoops, and many a time it seemed they heard them. In the midst of their nervous terror it was often a sore temptation to consult old Goody Crane, since she was held to have occult knowledge.

"I'll warrant old Goody Crane could tell us in a twinkling whether or no the Indians would come before morning," Eunice Bishop said one fierce windy night that called to mind the one of the massacre.

"Knowledge got in unlawful ways would avail us naught," returned Goodwife Spear. "I trow the Lord be yet able to protect His people."

"I doubt not that," said Eunice Bishop, "but I would like well to know if I had best bury my hood and my spinning-wheel and looking-glass in a snow-drift to-night. I have no mind the Indians shall get them. I warrant she knows well."

But Eunice Bishop did not consult Goody Crane, although she watched her narrowly and had a sharp ear to her mutterings as she sat in the chimney-corner. Eunice and Silence were living in John Sheldon's house, as did many of the survivors for some time after the massacre. It was the largest house in the village, and most of its original inhabitants were dead or gone into captivity. The people all huddled together fearfully in the few houses that were left, and the women's spinning-wheels and looms jostled each other.

As soon as the weather moderated, the work of building new dwellings commenced, and went on bravely with the advance of the spring. The air was full of the calls of spring birds and the strokes of axes and hammers. A little house was built on the site of their old one for Widow Bishop and Silence Hoit. Widow Sarah Spear also lived with them, and Goody Crane took frequent shelter at their fireside. So they were

a household of women, with loaded muskets at
hand, and spinning-wheels and looms at full
hum. They had but a scanty household store,
although Widow Bishop tried in every way to in-
crease it. Several times during the summer she
took perilous journeys to Hatfield and Squak-
heak, for the purpose of bartering skeins of yarn
or rolls of wool for household articles. In De-
cember, when Ensign Sheldon with young Freedom Wells went down to Boston to consult with
Governor Dudley concerning an expedition to
Canada to redeem the captives, Widow Eunice
Bishop, having saved a few shillings, burdened
him with a commission to purchase for her a
new cap and a pair of bellows. She was much
angered when he returned without them, having
quite forgotten them in his press of business.

On the day when John Sheldon and Freedom
Wells started upon their terrible journey of
three hundred miles to redeem the captives,
Eunice Bishop scolded well as she spun by her
hearth fire.

"I trow they will bring back nobody," said
she, her nose high in air, and her voice shrilling
over the drone of the wheel; "an they could not
do the bidding of a poor lone widow-woman,
and fetch her the cap and bellows from Boston,
they'll fetch nobody home from Canada. I
would I had ear of Governor Dudley. I trow
men with minds upon their task would be sent."

Eunice kept jerking her head as she scolded, and spun like a bee angry with its own humming.

Silence sat knitting, and paid no heed. She had paid no heed to any of the talk about Ensign Sheldon's and Freedom Wells's journey to Canada. She had not seemed to listen when Widow Spear had tried to explain the matter to her. "It may be, sweetheart, if it be the will of the Lord, that they will bring David back to thee," she had said over and over, and Silence had knitted and made no response.

She was the only one in Deerfield who was not torn with excitement and suspense as the months went by, and the only one unmoved by joy or disappointment when in May John Sheldon and Freedom Wells returned with five of the captives. But David Walcott was not among them.

"Said I not 'twould be so?" scolded Eunice Bishop. "Knew I not 'twould be so when they forgot to get the cap and the bellows in Boston? The one of all the captives that could have saved a poor maid's wits they leave behind. There's Mary Sheldon come home, and she a-coloring red before Freedom Wells, and everybody in the room a-seeing it. I trow they might have done somewhat for poor Silence," and Eunice broke down and wailed and wept, but Silence shed not a tear. Before long she stole out to the terrace and called "David! David!

David !" over the north meadow, and strained her blue eyes towards Canada, and held out her fair arms, but it was with no new disappointment and desolation.

There was never a day nor a night that Silence called not over the north meadow like a spring bird from the bush to her absent mate, and people heard her and sighed and shuddered. One afternoon in the last of the month of June, as Silence was thrusting her face between the leaves of a wild cherry-tree and calling " David ! David ! David !" David himself broke through the thicket and stood before her. He and three other young men had escaped from their captivity and come home, and the four, crawling half dead across the meadow, had heard Silence's voice from the terrace above, and David, leaving the others, had made his way to her.

"Silence !" he said, and held out his poor arms, panting.

But Silence looked past him. "David! David! David Walcott !" she called.

David could scarcely stand for trembling, and he grasped a branch of the cherry-tree to steady himself, and swayed with it.

" Know—you not—who I am, Silence ?" he said.

But she made as though she did not hear, and called again, always looking past him. And David Walcott, being near spent with fatigue

SILENCE

and starvation, wound himself feebly around the
trunk of the tree, and the tears dropped over his
cheeks as he looked at her; and she called past
him, until some women came and led him away
and tried to comfort him, telling him how it was
with her, and that she would soon know him
when he looked more like himself.

But the summer wore away and she did not
know him, although he constantly followed her
beseechingly. His elders even reproved him for
paying so little heed to his work in the colony.
"It is not meet for a young man to be so weaned
from usefulness by grief for a maid," said they.
But David Walcott would at any time leave his
reaping-hook in the corn and his axe in the tree,
leave aught but his post as sentry, when he heard
Silence calling him over the north meadow. He
would stand at her elbow and say, in his voice
that broke like a woman's: "Here I am, sweetheart, at thy side. I pray thee turn thy head."
But she would not let her eyes rest upon him
for more than a second's space, turning them
ever past him towards Canada, and calling in his
very ears with a sad longing that tore his heart:
"David! David! David!" It was as if her
mind, reaching out always and speeding fast in
search of him, had gotten such impetus that she
passed the very object of her search and knew it
not.

Now and then would David Walcott grow des-

48

perate, fling his arms around her, and kiss her upon her cold delicate lips and cheeks as if he would make her recognize him by force ; but she would free herself from him with a passionless resentment that left him helpless.

One day in autumn, when the borders of the Deerfield meadows were a smoky purple with wild asters, and golden-rods flashed out like golden flames in the midst of them, David Walcott had been pleading vainly with Silence as she stood calling on the north terrace. Suddenly he turned and rushed away, and his face was all convulsed like a weeping child's. As he came out of the thicket he met the old woman Goody Crane, and would fain have hidden his face from her, but she stopped him.

" Prithee stop a moment's space, Master David Walcott," said she.

"What would you?" David cried out in a surly tone, and he dashed the back of his hand across his eyes.

" 'Tis full moon to-night," said the old woman, in a whisper. " Come out here to-night when the moon shall be an hour high, and I promise ye she shall know ye."

The young man stared at her.

" I tell ye Mistress Silence Hoit shall know ye to-night," repeated the old woman. Her voice sounded hollow in the depths of her great hood, which she donned early in the fall. Her eyes in the gloom of it gleamed with a small dark brightness.

"I'll have no witch-work tried on her," said David, roughly.

"I'll try no witch-work but mine own wits," said Goody Crane. "If they would hang me for a witch for that, then they may. None but I can cure her. I tell ye, come out here to-night when the moon is an hour high; and mind ye wear a white sheep's fleece over your shoulders. I'll harm her not so much with my witch-work as ye'll do with your love, for all your prating."

The old woman pushed past him to where Silence stood calling, and waited there, standing in the shadow cast by the wild cherry-tree until she ceased and turned away. Then she caught hold of the skirt of her gown, and David stood, hidden by the thicket, listening.

"I prithee, Mistress Silence Hoit, listen but a moment," said Goody Crane.

Silence paused, and smiled at her gently and wearily.

"Give me your hand," demanded the old woman.

And Silence held out her hand, flashing white in the green gloom, as if she cared not.

The old woman turned the palm, bending her hooded head low over it. "He draweth near!" she cried out suddenly; "he draweth near, with

a white sheep's fleece over his shoulders! He
cometh through the woods from Canada. He
will cross the meadow when the moon is an hour
high to-night. He will wear a white sheep's
fleece over his shoulders, and ye'll know him by
that."

Silence's wandering eyes fastened upon her
face.

The old woman caught hold of her shoulders
and shook her to and fro. "David! David!
David Walcott!" she screamed. "David Walcott with a white sheep's fleece on his back! On
the meadow! To-night when the moon's an
hour high! Be ye out here to-night, Silence
Hoit, if ye'd see him a-coming down from the
north!"

Silence gasped faintly when the old woman re-
leased her and went muttering away. Presently
she crept home, and sat down with her knitting-
work in the chimney-place.

When Eunice Bishop hung on the porridge-
kettle, Goody Crane lifted the latch-string and
came in. It was growing dusky, but the moon
would not rise for an hour yet. Goody Crane
sat opposite Silence, with her eyes fixed upon
her, and Silence, in spite of herself, kept looking at her. A gold brooch at the old woman's
throat glittered in the firelight, and that seemed
to catch Silence's eyes. She finally knitted with
them fixed upon it.

She scarcely took her eyes away when she ate her supper; then she sat down to her knitting and knitted, and gazed, in spite of herself, at the gold spot on the old woman's throat.

The moon arose; the tree branches before the windows tossed half in silver light; the air was shrill with crickets. Silence stirred uneasily, and dropped stitches in her knitting-work. "He draweth near," muttered Goody Crane, and Silence quivered.

The moon was a half-hour high. Widow Bishop was spinning, Widow Spear was winding quills, and Silence knitted. "He draweth near," muttered Goody Crane.

"I'll have no witchcraft!" Silence cried out, suddenly and sharply. Her aunt stopped spinning, and Widow Spear started.

"What's that?" said her aunt. But Silence was knitting again.

"What meant you by that?" asked her aunt, sharply.

"I have dropped a stitch," said Silence.

Her aunt spun again, with occasional wary glances. The moon was three-quarters of an hour high. Silence gazed steadily at the gold brooch at Goody Crane's throat.

"The moon is near an hour high; you had best be going," said the old woman, in a low monotone.

Silence arose directly.

"Where go you at this time of night?" grumbled her aunt. But Silence glided past her.

"You'll lose your good name as well as your wits," cried Eunice. But she did not try to stop Silence, for she knew it was useless.

"A white sheep's fleece over his shoulders," muttered Goody Crane as Silence went out of the door; and the other women marvelled what she meant.

Silence Hoit went swiftly and softly down Deerfield street to her old haunt on the north meadow terrace. She pushed in among the wild cherry-trees, which waved, white with the moonlight, like ghostly arms in her face. Then she called, setting her face towards Canada and the north: "David! David! David!" But her voice had a different tone in it, and it broke with her heart-beats.

David Walcott came slowly across the meadow below; a white fleece of a sheep thrown over his back caught the moonlight. He came on, and on, and on; then he went up the terrace to Silence. Her face, white like a white flower in the moonlight, shone out suddenly close before him. He waited a second, then he spoke. "Silence!" he said.

Then Silence gave a great cry, and threw her arms around his neck, and pressed softly and wildly against him with her wet cheek to his.

"Know you who 'tis, sweetheart?"

" Oh, David, David !"

The trees arched like arbors with the weight of the wild grapes, which made the air sweet; the night insects called from the bushes; Deerfield village and the whole valley lay in the moonlight like a landscape of silver. The lovers stood in each other's arms, motionless, and seemingly fixed as the New England flora around them, as if they too might reappear hundreds of spring-times hence, with their loves as fairly in blossom.

THE BUCKLEY LADY

THE dark slate stones that now slant to their falls in the old burying-ground, or are fallen already, then stood straight. The old inscriptions, now blurred over by moss and lichen, or worn back into the face of the stone by the wash of the heavy coast rains, were then quite plain. The winged cherubim and death-heads—the terrible religious symbols of the Old Testament, made realistic by New England minds under stress of grief—were quite fresh from the artist's hands.

The funeral urns and weeping-willows, a very art of sorrow in themselves, with their every curve the droop of a mourner's head, and all their flowing lines of tears, were still distinct. Indeed, the man who had graven many of them was still alive, and not yet past his gloomy toil. He lived in his little house not far beyond the burying-ground, and his name was Ichabod Buckley. He had a wife Sarah, a son Ichabod, and three daughters, Submit, Rebecca, and Persis. When Persis was twelve years old a great change and a romance came into her life. She was the youngest of the family; her brother was ten years older than she; her sisters were older still. She had always been to a certain extent petted and favored from her babyhood; however, until she was twelve, she had not been exempt from her own little duties and privations. She had gathered drift-wood on the shore, her delicate little figure buffeted and shaken by rough winds. She had dug quahaugs, wading out in the black mud, with her petticoats kilted high over her slender childish legs. She had spun her daily stint, and knitted faithfully harsh blue yarn socks for her father and brother. In the early autumn, when she was twelve years old, all that was changed.

One morning in September it was hot inland, but cool on the point of land reaching out into the sea where the Buckley house stood. The son, Ichabod, had gone to sea in a whaling-vessel; the father was at home, working in the little slanting shed behind the house. One could hear the grating slide of his chisel down the boughs of a weeping-willow on a new grave-stone. A very old woman of the village had died that week.

At the left of the house there was a bright unexpected glint from a great brass kettle which the eastern sun struck. Ichabod Buckley's wife had her dye-kettle out there on forked sticks over a fire. She was dyeing some cloth an indigo-blue, and her two elder daughters were helping her. The two daughters Submit and Rebecca looked like their mother. The three, from their figures, seemed about of an age—all tall and meagre and long-limbed, moving in their scanty petticoats around the kettle with a certain dry pliability, like three tall brown weeds on the windy marsh.

Persis came up from the shore at the front of the house with her arms full of drift-wood. She was just crossing the front yard when she heard a sound that startled her, and she stood still and listened, inclining her head towards the woods on the right. In the midst of these woods was the cleared space of the graveyard; the rough path to the main road ran past it.

Seldom any but horseback riders came that way; but now Persis was sure that she heard the rumble of carriage-wheels, as well as the tramp of horses' feet. She turned excitedly to run to her mother and sisters; but all at once the splendid coach and four emerged with a great flourish on the open space before the house, and she stood still.

The short coarse grass in the yard had gotten a perpetual slant from the wind. Just now it was still, but that low bending sweep of the grass towards the west made it seem as if the

wind were transfixed there. Persis stood in the
midst of this still show of wind, her slender
childish figure slanting a little also. All her
fair hair was tucked away tidily beneath a little
blue hood tied under her chin. The oval of her
face showed like the oval of a pearl in this circle
of blue, and it had a beauty that could draw the
thoughts of people away from their own hearts.
Even the folk of this old New England village,
who had in their stern doctrines no value for a
fair face, turned for a second, as if by some com-
pelling gleam of light under their eyelids, when
this little Buckley maid entered the meeting-
house; and her mother and sisters, although
they saw her every day, would stop sometimes
their work or speech when her face came suddenly before their eyes.

Persis had her little looking-glass. She looked
in it when she had washed her face to see if it
were clean, and when she braided her hair to see
if it were smooth. Sometimes she paused, herself, and eyed her face with innocent wonder,
but she did not know its value. She was like a
child with a precious coin which had its equiva-
lent in goods beyond her ken.

To-day Persis had no idea why these fine strangers in the grand coach sat still with their eyes
riveted upon her face.

She stood there in the windy grass, in her little straight blue gown, clasping her bundle of

drift-wood to her breast, and stared, turning her back altogether upon her own self, at the coach and the trappings, and the black coachman in his livery, with his head like a mop of black sheep's wool, and his white rolling eyes, which half frightened her. She looked a little more curiously at this black coachman than at the gentleman and lady in the coach, although they were grand enough ; and, moreover, the gentleman was very handsome, and not old. He thrust his fair head, which had a slight silvery sheen of powder, out of the coach window, and the pale old face and velvet hood of the lady showed over his shoulder, and they both stared at Persis's face.

Then the gentleman spoke, and Persis started, and blushed, and dropped a courtesy. She had forgotten that until now, and felt overcome with shame. " Good-day, my pretty maid," said the gentleman ; and as he spoke he stepped out of the coach and approached Persis. She saw, with half-dazzled eyes, his grand fair head, his queue tied with a blue silk ribbon, his jewelled knee-buckles and silk hose, his flowered waist-coat, and the deep falls of lace over his long white hands. No such fine gentleman as this had ever come within her vision. She courtesied again, and looked up in his face when he reached her. Then she looked down again quickly, and the strange salt savor of the drift-

wood, overpowering a sweet perfume about the
stranger's rich attire, came up in her blushing
face. The gentleman looked very kind, and his
eyes were very gay and blue, yet somehow she
was frightened and abashed. It was as if he
saw something within herself of which she had
not dreamed, and suddenly forced her to see it
also, to her own confusion.

The gentleman laughed softly when she looked
down. "Is it the first time you have had another pair of eyes for your looking-glass, little
maid?" he asked, with a kind of mocking caress
in his tone.

Persis did not lift her eyes from the drift-
wood. She blushed more deeply, and her sweet
mouth trembled.

"Nay, tease not the child. Ask if her father
be in the house," called the lady's soft voice,
with a little impatient ring in it, from the
coach.

"'Tis but the fault of my eyes, your lady-
ship," retorted the gentleman, gayly. "They
are ever as lakes reflecting flowers in the presence of beauty, and I doubt much if this little
maid hath ever seen herself so clearly before—if
eyes like mine have come in her way."

Persis's mouth quivered more. She wanted to
run away, and did not dare; but suddenly the
gentleman spoke again, quite gravely and coldly, and all the gay banter in his voice was gone.

"Is your father, Ichabod Buckley, within, my good maid?" he said.

Persis felt as if a spell which had been cast over her were broken. She dropped a courtesy.

"Please, sir, my father is yonder, cutting a weeping-willow on old Widow Nye's gravestone," she replied, pointing towards the rear of the house; and she spoke with that punctilious courtesy with which she had been taught to address strangers.

"Will you bid him come this way? I would speak with him," said the gentleman.

"And bid him hasten, for this air from the sea is full cold for me!" called the lady from the coach.

Persis dipped another affirmative courtesy towards her, then fled swiftly around the corner of the house. She met her mother and her sister Submit face to face, with a shock. They had been peeping around the corner at the grand folk. Rebecca had run into the house to put on her shoes and a clean kerchief, in case one of the elder women had to go forward to speak to them.

"Father! the gentleman wants father," said Persis, with soft pants. "Oh, mother!"

Her mother caught her arm with a jerk. "Who be they?" she hissed in her ear.

"I—don't know—such—grand folks, and—the coach and the four, and the black man—oh, mother!"

"Go bid your father come quick."

Sarah Buckley gave her daughter a push, and Persis flew on towards the shed where her father kept his stock of gravestones and worked. But Rebecca had already given him the alarm, and he was at the well washing the slate dust from his hands.

"Go quick, father; they want you!" panted Persis.

"Who be they?" queried Ichabod Buckley. His voice was as nervous as a woman's, and he was small and delicately made like one. He shook the water from his small hands, his fingers twitching. The muscles on the backs glanced under the thin brown skin; the muscles on his temples and neck glanced also. Ichabod Buckley had, when nervously excited, a look as if his whole body were based on a system of brown wires.

Persis danced up and down before him, as if his nervous excitement communicated itself to her. "I know not who they be," she panted; "but, oh, father, they be such grand folk!"

When Ichabod Buckley, striving to pace with solemn dignity, as befitted his profession, but breaking, in spite of himself, into nervous runs, went around to the front of the house, Persis slunk at his heels, but her mother arrested her at the corner. "Stay where you be, and not go out there staring at the gentle-folk like a bold

hussy!" she ordered. So Persis stayed, peeping
around the corner with her mother and Submit;
and presently Rebecca in her shoes, with her
kerchief pinned over her lean bosom, joined
them.

Once Persis, advancing her beautiful face a
little farther around the corner, caught the
gentleman's gay blue eyes full upon her, and she
drew back with a great start and a blush.

Listen as they might, the women could not
catch one word of Ichabod Buckley's and the
gentleman's discourse—they stood too far away.
But presently they saw the black coachman turn
the coach and four around with a wide careful
sweep, and then the gentleman got in beside the
lady, and Ichabod beside the coachman, and
then the horses leaped forward, and the whole
was out of sight behind the spray of pine woods.

Ichabod Buckley was gone about three-quarters of an hour. When he returned he at once
told his curious women-folks somewhat that
had passed, but his face was locked over more.
"You have not told us all," said his wife, sharply. "It may well be, as you say, that the gentle-
folk wished to find the grave of the man who
was their kin, and died here in the first of the
town, but that is not all."

"I pointed out the grave to them beyond a
question," said Ichabod, "though there was no

stone to it. I knew it well from hearsay. And I am to make at once a fine stone, with a round top and a winged head, and here is the pay already."

Ichabod jingled for the dozenth time a gold coin and some small silver ones in his nervous hand, and his wife frowned.

"You have told us all this before," said she. "There is something else that you keep back."

Ichabod was smiling importantly, he could not control his mouth; but he went back without another word to old Widow Nye's gravestone, and the weeping-willow thereon grew apace under his hands.

However, he could not keep anything to himself long, least of all from his wife, with her imperative curiosity. After dinner that noon he beckoned her into the front room.

"What do you want of me?" she said. "I have the work to do." She felt that his previous silence demanded some show of dignity upon her part.

Ichabod glanced at his staring daughters, and beckoned beseechingly.

"Well, I can't waste much time," said Sarah; but she followed him eagerly into the front room. They were shut in there some time. The daughters, tidying up the kitchen, could hear the low murmur of their parents' voices, but that was all. Persis was polishing the

brasses on the hearth — the andirons and the
knobs on the shovel and tongs. That was always her task. It roughened her small hands,
but nobody ever minded that. To-day, as she
was scouring away sturdily, her mother came
suddenly out of the front room and caught her
plying arm.

"There!" said she; "you need do no more of
this. 'Twill get your hands all out of shape,
and make them rough. They are too small for
such work. Submit, come here and finish
scouring the brasses."

Persis looked up at her mother and then at
her little red grimy hands in a bewildered way.

"Go and wash your hands, and then rub
some Injun meal on them, and see if it will not
make them a little softer," ordered her mother.
"Submit, make haste."

Submit, although she was herself puzzled, and
might well have been resentful, knelt obediently down on the hearth, and fell to work on
the brasses, rubbing vigorously with salt and
vinegar.

Persis washed her hands as her mother bade
her, and afterwards rubbed on some Indian meal.
Then she was ordered to put on her pink-flowered
chintz gown, and sit down in the front room
with her sampler. Her mother braided her fair
hair for her in two tight smooth braids, and
crossed them neatly at the back. She even put

her own beautiful high tortoise-shell comb in her daughter's head.

"You may wear it a spell if you want to," said she.

Persis smiled delightedly. Her chief worldly ambition had been to wear a shell comb like her mother's.

The window was open. She could hear faintly the rasp of her father's chisel upon the boughs of old Widow Nye's weeping-willow. She could hear the voices of her mother and sisters, who had gone back to their work over the dye-kettle. After a while she saw Submit going down to the shore for more drift-wood. "That is my work," she thought to herself with wonder. She could not understand her mother's treatment of her. It was very pleasant and grand to be sitting in state in the best room, with the tortoise-shell comb in her hair, working her sampler, and be rid of all ruder toil, yet she finally grew uneasy.

She laid down her sampler, and pulled open the front door, which was seldom used, and hard to move, being swollen with the sea dampness. Then she stole around the house towards the group at the dye-kettle. She felt scared and uncertain without knowing why. Her mother called out sharply when she caught sight of her, and waved her back. "Can't I go down for more drift-wood?" pleaded Persis, timidly.

"Back into the house !" ordered her mother, speaking against the wind, which was now blowing hard. "Back with ye ! Out here in this wind ! Would you be as black as an Injun ? Go back to your sampler !"

Persis crept back, bewildered. The other two daughters looked at each other. Then Rebecca spoke out boldly.

"Mother, what is all this ?" said she.

"Perhaps you will know sometime," replied Sarah Buckley, smiling mysteriously, and she would say no more.

Persis continued to sit at the front-room window with her sampler in her hands. She cross-stitched a letter forlornly and laboriously, with frequent glances out at the rosy wind-swept marshes and the blue dazzle of sea beyond. She never dreamed of disputing her mother's wishes further. Persis Buckley, although full of nervous force, had also a strange docility of character. She stitched on her sampler all the afternoon. When it came time to prepare supper, her mother would not even then let her out in the kitchen to help, as was her wont. "Stay where you be," said she, when Persis appeared on the threshold. And the little maid remained in her solitary state until the meal was ready, and she was bidden forth to it. There was a little sweet cake beside her plate on the table, one of those which her mother kept in a stone jar for company. Nobody else had one. Persis looked at it doubtfully when she had finished her bread. "Eat it," said her mother, and Persis ate it, but it tasted strange to her. She wondered if her mother had put anything different in the sweet cake.

Persis had lately sat up until the nine-o'clock bell rang, knitting or paring sweet apples to dry, but now her mother sent her off to bed at half past seven.

"Can't I sit up and help Submit and Rebecca pare apples?" she begged, but her mother was inexorable.

"I am not going to have your hands spoilt with apple juice," said she. "Besides, if you go to bed early 'twill make you grow faster and keep your cheeks red." There was an unusual softness in Sarah Buckley's voice, and she colored and smiled foolishly, as if she were ashamed of it.

Ichabod Buckley sat on the hearth whittling chips with lightning jerks of his clasp-knife. He did everything swiftly. "Do as your mother bids you," he said to Persis. He chuckled nervously, and looked meaningly at his wife.

Persis went laggingly out of the room.

"Stand up straight," ordered her mother. "The first thing you know you'll be all bent over like an old woman."

Persis threw back her weak girlish shoulders until her slender back hollowed. She had been trained to obedience. She clattered slowly up the stairs in her little heavy shoes, still trying to keep her shoulders back, when her mother called again.

"Come back here, Persis," called her mother, and Persis returned to the kitchen. "Sit down here," said her mother, pointing to a chair, and Persis sat down. She did not ask any questions; she felt a curious terror and intimidation. She waited, sitting meekly with her eyes cast down. She heard the snip of shears and the rattle of stiff paper at her back, then she felt a sharp tug at her hair. She winced a little.

"You keep still," said her mother at her back, rolling a lock of hair vigorously. "I ain't going to have your hair as straight as a broom if I can help it."

When Persis went to bed her head was covered with hard papered knots of hair, all straining painfully at the roots. When she laid her head uncomfortably on her pillow, she remembered in a bewildered way how her mother had smoothed and smoothed and smoothed her hair in former days, and how she had said many a time that rough and frowsly locks were not modest or becoming. Her first conviction of the inconsistency of the human heart was upon little Persis Buckley, and she was dazed. The whole of this strange experience did not seem real enough to last until the next day.

But the days went on and on, and she continued to live a life as widely different from her old one as if she had been translated into another world. She sat at the front-room window, with her beautiful face looking out meekly from under her crown of curl-papers. Her mother had a theory that a long persistency in the use of the papers might produce a lasting curl, and Persis was seldom freed from them. She walked abroad on a pleasant day at a genteel pace, with a thick black embroidered veil over her face to protect her complexion. She never ran barefoot, and even her thick cowhide shoes were discarded. She wore now dainty high-heeled red morocco shoes, which made her set her feet down as delicately as some little pink-footed pigeon. All her coarse home-spun gowns were laid away in a chest. She wore now fine chintz or soft boughten wool of a week-day, and she even had a gown of silken stuff and a fine silk pelisse for Sabbath days.

Going into the meeting-house beside her soberly clad parents and sisters, she looked like some gay-feathered bird which had somehow gotten into the wrong nest. All the Buckley family seemed to have united in a curious reversed tyranny towards this beautiful child. She was set up as a queen among them, whether she would or no, and she was made to take the best in their lot, whether she wanted it or not.

When Persis was fourteen, her sister Rebecca went some fifty miles away to keep house for a widowed uncle and take care of his family of children. She was not needed at home, and in this way the cost of her support was saved for Persis. Submit was a dull woman, and hard work was making her duller. She broadened her patient back for her own and her sister's burdens without a murmur, and became a contented drudge that Persis might sit in state in the front room, keeping her hands soft and white.

As for Persis's brother Ichabod, nearly all his savings were given to her, but, after all, not with any especial self-denial. This beautiful young sister represented all the faint ambition in his life; he had none left for himself, and nobody had tried to arouse any. He made perilous voyages on a whaling-ship for his living. When he came home, with his face browned and stiffened by his hard fight with the icy winds of the North Atlantic, he sat down by the fire in his father's kitchen. Then he chewed tobacco, and never stirred if he could help it until his next voyage.

At thirty, Ichabod had become as old as his father. All the dreams of youth had gone out of him, and he slumbered in the present like a very old man. Always as he sat chewing by the fire his face wore that look of set resistance, as if the lash of the North Atlantic wind still threatened it. Ever since she could remember, Persis Buckley had seen her brother sit there between his voyages, a dull reflective bulk before the hearth, like some figure-head of a stranded whaler.

The morning after his return from his voyage, Persis, passing her brother, would be arrested by an inarticulate command, and would pause while he dragged out his old leather bag, heavy with his hard-earned coins. Then Persis would hold up her apron by the two lower corners, and he would pour in a goodly portion of his wealth, while his face looked more smiling and animated than she ever saw it at any other time. "'Twill buy you something as good as anybody when you go among the grand folk," he would say, with a half-chuckle, when Persis thanked him.

Sarah Buckley hid away all this money for Persis in the till of the chest. "It will come handy some day," she would remark, with a meaning smile. This fund was not drawn upon for the purchase of Persis's daily needs and luxuries. Her father's earnings and her mother's thrift provided them, and with seemingly little stint. People said that the materials for Persis Buckley's crewel-work alone cost a pretty sum. After she had finished her sampler she worked a mourning-piece, and after that a great picture, all in cross-stitch, which was held to be a marvel.

Persis's very soul flagged over the house and

the green trees, the river, and the red rose-bushes, and the blue sky, all wrought with her needle, stitch by stitch. Once in the depths of her docile heart a sudden wish, which seemed as foreign to her as an impious spirit, leaped up that all this had never been created, since she was forced to reproduce it in cross-stitch.

"I wish," said Persis, quite out loud to herself when she was all alone in the front room— "I wish the trees had never been made, nor the roses, nor the river, nor the sky; then I shouldn't have had to work them." Then she fairly trembled at her wickedness, and counted the stitches in a corner of the sky with renewed zeal and faithfulness.

When Persis was sixteen, her mother, in her anxiety to provide her with accomplishments, went a step beyond all previous efforts, and a piano was bought for her. It was the very first piano which had ever come to this little seaport town. Ichabod had commissioned a sea-captain to purchase it in England.

When it was set up on its slender fluted legs in the Buckley front room, all the people came and craved permission to see it, and viewed its satiny surface and inlaid-work in mother-of-pearl with admiration and awe. Then they went away, and discoursed among themselves as to the folly and sinful extravagance of Ichabod Buckley and his wife.

There was in the village an ancient maiden lady who had lived in Boston in her youth, and had learned to play several tunes on the harpsichord. These, for a small stipend, she imparted to Persis. They were simple and artless melodies, and Persis had a ready ear. In a short time she had learned all the maiden lady knew. She could sing three old songs, innocently imitating her teacher's quaver with her sweet young voice, and she could finger out quite correctly one battle piece and two jigs. The two jigs she played very slowly, according to her teacher's instructions. Persis herself did not know why, but this elderly maiden was astute. She did not wish Ichabod Buckley and his family to be tormented with scruples themselves, neither did she wish to be called to account for teaching light and worldly tunes.

"Play these very slowly, my dear," she said. She shook the two bunches of gray curls which bobbed outside her cap over her thin red cheeks; her old blue eyes winked with a light which Persis did not understand.

"Be they psalm tunes?" she inquired, innocently.

"'Tis according to the way you play them," replied her teacher, evasively.

And Persis never knew, nor any of her family, that she played jigs. However, one worldly amusement, which was accounted distinctly sin-

ful, was Persis taught with the direct connivance
of her parents.

This old maiden lady, although she was constant in the meeting-house on the Sabbath day,
and was not seen to move a muscle of dissent
when the parson proclaimed the endless doom of
the wicked, had Unitarian traditions, and her
life in her youth had been more gayly and broadly ordered than that of those about her. It had
always been whispered that she had played
cards, and had even danced, in days gone by.
To the most rigidly sanctified nostrils there was
always perceptible a faint spiritual odor of past
frivolity when she came into the meeting-house,
although she seemed to subscribe faithfully to
all the orthodox tenets. The parson often felt
it his duty to call upon her, and enter into
wordy expounding of the truth, and tempt her
with argument. She never questioned his precepts, and never argued, yet a suspicion as to
her inmost heresy was always abroad. Had it
not been so, Sarah Buckley would never have
dared make one proposition to her with regard
to her daughter's accomplishments.

One day the shutters in the Buckley front
room were carefully closed, as if some one lay
dead therein ; the candles were lighted, and this
ancient maiden lady, holding with both hands
her petticoats above her thin ankles in their
black silk hose, taught Persis Buckley some dan-

cing steps. That, nobody in the village ever knew. All the parties concerned would have been brought before the church had that secret been disclosed. The Buckleys scarcely dared mention it to one another.

This old teacher of Persis Buckley had still some relatives left in Boston, and now and then she went to them on a visit. On one of these occasions Sarah Buckley commissioned her to purchase some books for Persis. All the literature in the Buckley house consisted of the Bible, Watts's Hymns, and Doddridge's *Rise and Progress*, and Sarah fancied that another book or two of possibly an ornamental and decorative tendency might be of use in her daughter's education.

When Mistress Tabitha Hopkins returned from Boston she brought with her a volume of Young's *Night Thoughts* and one of Richardson's *Clarissa Harlowe*. The first she presented with confidence, the second with some excuses.

"I know well that the poetry is of a nature that will elevate her soul and tend to form her mind," said she, "and I have myself no doubt as to the other. If it be a tale, 'tis one she can read to her profit, and the pleasure she may take in it may lead her to peruse it more closely. 'Tis well sometimes to season hard doctrines with sugar if you would have them gulped down at all." Mistress Hopkins made a wry face, as if

the said doctrines were even then like bitter pills
in her mouth, and Sarah Buckley glanced at
her suspiciously. However, she took the books,
and paid for them a goodly sum, and Persis was
henceforth made acquainted with the lofty ad-
monitions to Lorenzo and the woes of the unfortunate and virtuous Clarissa.

It might well have been that Tabitha Hopkins's recommendation of the story of poor
Clarissa Harlowe and her desperate experience at
the hands of a faithless lover had its object.
Mistress Tabitha Hopkins's single life had not
predisposed her to implicit reliance upon the
good faith or the motives of gay gallants who, in
the course of some little trip out of their world,
chanced to notice a beautiful rustic maiden.
Everybody in the village knew now the reason
for Ichabod Buckley's and his wife's strange
treatment of their daughter Persis. They knew
that the grand gentleman who had come to town
with the coach and four had seen Persis, and
cried out at her beauty, and made her father
give his promise that she should be kept for him
until she was grown up, when he would come
over seas from England and marry her.

Ichabod had vainly tried to keep this secret,
but he had told it before a week had passed to
old Thomas Knapp, who was helping him to set
Widow Nye's gravestone.

Then the sun had not set before the news was

widely spread. Marvellous tales were told of
this gentleman and his lady mother, who had
come in the coach with him. Persis, when she
was wedded, would dwell in marble halls, wear
satin and velvet of a week-day, and eat off gold
and silver dishes. No wonder that Ichabod
Buckley and his wife Sarah were doing their
poor best to fit their daughter for such a high
estate! No wonder that they kept her all day
in the best room embroidering and reading
poetry and playing music! No wonder that
they never let her walk abroad without morocco
shoes and a veil over her face!

"It ain't likely," said old man Knapp, "that
she'll ever have any call to so much as dye a
hank of yarn or dip a candle arter she's married."

Still, although people acquiesced in the wisdom of fitting Persis for this grand station, if
there were any prospect of her reaching it, they
were mostly incredulous or envious.

The incredulous said quite openly that Ichabod Buckley always did hear things five times as
big as they were, and they doubted much if the
grand gentleman ever really meant to or said he
would come back for Persis. The envious declared that if he did come they mistrusted that it
would not be for any good and honest purpose, for
he would never think Persis Buckley his equal,
in spite of all her fine accomplishments and her

gaudy attire. And her face might by that time
be no more beautiful than some others, after all.

The incredulous moved the parson to preach
many a discourse upon the folly of worldly ambition and trust in the vain promises of princes.
The envious instigated sermons upon the sin of
any other ornament or accomplishment than a
meek and quiet spirit for the daughters of Zion.

Poor little Persis, in her silken attire, lifting
her wonderful face to the parson, never dreamed
that the discourse was directed at her and her
parents, but Ichabod and Sarah knew, and sat
up with bristling stiffness. After that they
withdrew themselves largely from intercourse
with their neighbors. They felt as if the spiritual watch-dog had been set upon them, and they
were justly indignant. Sarah Buckley had always been given to staying at home and minding
the affairs of her own household; now she kept
herself more close than ever. Ichabod was by
nature sociable, and liked to fraternize with his
kind; but now almost his only dealing with
people outside his own family lay in his work
upon their gravestones.

The Buckleys lived by themselves in their
little house on the windy land past the graveyard, following out their own end in life, and all
the time were under a subtle spiritual bombard-
ment of doubt and envy and disapproval from
their neighbors in the village.

People talked much about Submit's patient drudgery, and felt for her the resentment which she did not feel for herself. "It is a shame the way they make that poor girl do all the work to keep her sister in idleness!" said they. They began to call Persis in derision "The Buckley Lady."

Poor Persis Buckley, shut out of the free air and away from all the mates of her youth, was leading the life of a forlorn princess in a fairy tale. She would have given all the money which her brother Ichabod brought her for his privilege of a cruise over the wild seas. Year after year she waited in her prison, cast about and bound, body and spirit, by the will and ambition of her parents, like steel cobwebs, for the prince who never came.

At first the romance of it all had appealed to her childish imagination. When the high destiny which awaited her had been disclosed, her heart leaped. She had been amused and pleased. She liked to watch out for that grand coach and four. When she remembered the gay blue flash of that grand gentleman's eyes she blushed, and laughed to herself.

But after a while all that failed. She did not grow incredulous, for she had a simple and long-suffering faith in her parents, but quietly and secretly frightened at the prospect before her. Poor Persis Buckley sometimes felt herself turn

fairly cold with dread at the thought of entering
that splendid coach and driving away forever
out of her old life at that strange gentleman's
side. He became to her as cold and formless as
a moving column of mist on the marsh, and
even the dreams which sprang of themselves in
her girlish heart could not invest him with love
and life again.

She did not dare confide her fears to her mother. Sometimes her mother filled her with a
vague alarm. Sarah Buckley in ten years grew
old, and the eagerness in her face waxed so
bright and sharp that one shrank before it involuntarily, as before some blinding on-coming
headlight of spirit.

All those years she waited and watched and
listened for that grand coach and four which
would bring her fortune in her daughter's. All
the ambition of her earthly life, largely balked
for herself, had centred in this. Her lot in the
world had been to tread out a ceaseless round of
sordid toil in her poor little home on the stormy
coast, but her beautiful daughter could take a
flight above it, and something of herself could
follow her.

She never gave up, although year after year
she watched and listened in vain : but finally her
body failed under this long strain of the spirit.
When Persis was twenty-three her mother died,
after a short illness. Then Persis found her

father as keen a guardian as her mother had been. Sarah had given him her farewell charges, and during her lifetime had imbued his nervous receptive nature with a goodly portion of her own spirit.

He wrought for his dead wife a fine tall stone, and set thereon a verse of his own composition. Ichabod Buckley was somewhat of a poet, publishing himself his effusions upon his gloomy stone pages. Then he fulfilled his own and her part towards their daughter Persis.

Sarah Buckley had been dead two years, and the Buckley Lady was twenty-five years old, sitting at her window in the front room, watching for the prince who never came.

"The fine gentleman will find an old maid waiting for him if he does not come before long," people said, with sniffs.

But Persis had really grown more and more beautiful. Her complexion, although she had lived so much within-doors, was not sickly, but pale and fine as a white lily. Her eyes were like dark stars, and her hair was a braided cap of gold, with light curls falling from it around her face and her sweet neck. Of late Persis had rebelled upon one minor point: she never, even of a morning, would sit at the window with her hair rolled up in curl-papers. She argued with her father, with a duplicity which was unlike her, that should the gentleman arrive suddenly, she would have no time to take them down before he saw her. But that was not the reason. Ichabod never suspected, neither did the stupid Submit, padding faithfully in her household tracks; the son, Ichabod, was away at sea. Nobody knew how the Buckley Lady, sitting in her window watching, had seen Darius Hopkins pass by, with never a coach and four, but striding bravely along on his own stalwart young legs, and how her heart had gone out to him and followed him, whether she would or not.

Darius Hopkins was Mistress Tabitha Hopkins's nephew, and he had come from Boston to pay his aunt a visit. People whispered that he had expectations, and had come with a purpose. Mistress Tabitha had received within two years a legacy, nobody knew how large, by the death of a relative. However that may have been, the young man treated his aunt with exceeding deference and tenderness. Her pride and delight were great. She held her head high, and swung out her slim foot with almost the motion of her old dancing steps when she went up the meeting-house aisle on a Sabbath day, leaning on her nephew's arm. Darius was finely dressed, and he was also a personable young man of whom she might well be proud. She kept glancing at him almost with the shy delight of a sweetheart. Darius had a glossy dark head and a dark complexion, but his eyes were blue and light, and somewhat, as she fondly thought, like her own.

Darius had arrived on a Thursday, and it was on that day Persis Buckley had seen him, and he had seen her at her window. Tabitha Hopkins's house was past the Buckleys', fairly out at sea, on the point, across the marshy meadows.

The young man glanced up carelessly at the Buckley house as he passed; then he started, and fairly stopped, and his heart leaped almost with fear, for it actually seemed to him that he saw the face of an angel in the window.

"Who was the maid in the window of the house back yonder?" he said to his aunt as soon as he had greeted her. He waved his hand carelessly backward, and tried to speak as carelessly, but his aunt gave him a sharp look.

"It must have been Persis Buckley," said she.

"There is not another face like that in the whole country," said the young man, and in spite of himself his tongue betrayed him.

"Yes, it is generally considered that she has a fair face," said Tabitha, dryly. "She has accomplishments also. She can play music, and she has a pretty voice for a song. She can dance, though that's not to be spoke of in this godly town, and she is well versed in polite literature. Persis Buckley is fitted to adorn any high estate to which she may be called."

There was a mysterious tone in Tabitha's voice, and her nephew looked at her with eager inquiry.

"What mean you, aunt?" he said.

"What I have said," replied she, aggravatingly, and would tell him no more. She was secretly a little jealous that her nephew had shortened his greeting to her to inquire about Persis. Old single woman though she was, her feminine birthright of jealousy of the love of men, be they lovers or sons or nephews, still survived in her heart.

The young man dared not ask her any more questions, but the next day he passed the Buckley house many a time with sidelong glances at the window where Persis sat. He would not stare too boldly at that fair vision. And in the evening he stole out and strolled slowly over the meadows, and came to the Buckley house again. She was not at the window then, but the sweet tinkle of her piano came out to him from the candle-lit room, and he listened in rapture to her tender little voice trilling and quavering. Then peeping cautiously, he saw her graceful head thrown back, and her white throat swelling with her song like a bird's.

When he returned, his aunt looked at him sharply, but she did not ask where he had been. When he took his candle to retire for the night, her old blue eyes twinkled at him suddenly.

" How did the little bird sing to-night ?" she said.

The young man stared at her a second, then he blushed and laughed. " Bravely, aunt, bravely," he replied.

" 'Tis a bird in the bush, nephew," said she, and her voice was mocking, yet shrewdly tender.

Darius's face fell. " What do you mean, aunt ?" he said.

" 'Tis a bird that will always sing in the bush, and never in hand."

Darius made as if he would question his aunt further, but he did not. He bade her good-night in a downcast and confused manner, and was out of the room like a shy girl.

Mistress Tabitha chuckled to herself, then she looked grave, and sat in her rocking-chair for a long time thinking.

Darius Hopkins marvelled much what his aunt could mean by her warning, and was uneasy over it. But the next day also he had many an errand across the meadows, down the forest road, to the village, and always he saw, without seeming to see, Persis at the window, and always she saw, without seeming to see, him.

On the Sabbath day, when he and his aunt went by the Buckley house on their way to meeting, Persis was not at the window. His aunt surprised his sly glances. " They go to meeting early," said she, demurely. Darius laughed in a shamefaced fashion.

After he and his aunt were seated in the meeting-house, he scarcely dared look up for a while. for he feared, should he see Persis suddenly and near at hand, his face might alter in spite of himself. And, in truth, when he did look up. and saw Persis close before him in a pew at the side of the pulpit, a tremor ran over him, his lips twitched, and all the color left his face. His aunt pressed her bottle of salts into his hand, and he pressed it back almost sharply, and turned red as a girl to the roots of his black hair. Then he sat up straight and looked over almost defiantly at Persis. Her face in her blue satin bonnet, with its drooping blue plume and lace veil thrown to one side, was fair enough to stir the heart of any mortal man who looked at her.

There were, indeed, in that meeting-house, certain godly men who kept their eyes sternly turned away, and would not look upon her, thinking it a sin, although it was a sin to their own hearts alone.

But many a young man besides Darius Hopkins, although he had seen her in that selfsame place Sabbath after Sabbath, still regarded her furtively with looks of almost startled adoration. Not one of them had ever spoken to her or heard her speak, or seen her except in the meeting-house, or at her window, or thickly veiled on the village street.

Persis to-day kept her eyes fixed upon the parson, exhorting under his echoing sounding-board. She never looked around, although she knew that Darius was sitting beside his aunt in her pew. She also was afraid, and she never recovered courage, like Darius. Her father, Ichabod, fiercely intent upon the discourse, his nervous face screwed to a very point of attention, sat on one side : her sister Submit, her back bowed like an old woman's, on the other.

When meeting was over, Ichabod shot down the aisle, with his daughters following, as was his wont, and reached the door before many that sat farther back.

When Darius and his aunt came out of the meeting-house, the Buckleys were quite out of sight. When they emerged from the road past the graveyard through the woods, Persis was already at the window, with her bonnet off, but she kept her head turned far to one side, as if intent upon something in the room, and only the pink curve of one cheek was visible.

Darius had grown bold in the meeting-house ; this time he looked, and forgot himself in looking.

"She is a pretty maid, but she is not for you, nor for any other young man unless he come for her with a coach and four, with a black gentleman a-driving," said his aunt's voice half mockingly at his side.

Then the young man turned and questioned her quite boldly. " I beg of you to tell me what you mean, aunt," he said.

Then Mistress Tabitha Hopkins, holding her Sabbath gown high above her hooped satin petticoat as she stepped along, unfolded to her nephew Darius Hopkins the strange romance of Persis Buckley's life.

" 'Tis a shame !" cried the young man, indignantly, when she had finished — " a shame, to keep her a prisoner in this fashion !"

" 'Tis only a prince with a coach and four can set her free. A prince from over seas, with a black gentleman a-driving," said his aunt.

Darius turned, and stared back across the flat meadow-land at Ichabod Buckley's house. It was late August now, and the meadow had great rosy patches of marsh - rosemary flung upon it like silken cloaks of cavaliers, and far - seen purple plumes of blazing - star. Darius studied slowly the low gray walls and long slant of gray roofs in the distance.

" A strong right arm and a willing heart might free her, were he prince or not !" said he. And he flung out his own right arm as if it were the one to do it.

" Were the maid willing to be freed," said Mistress Tabitha, softly.

Darius' colored. "That is true, aunt," he said, with a downcast and humbled air, and he turned and went on soberly.

Mistress Tabitha looked at her nephew's handsome face, and thought to herself, with loving but jealous pride, that no maid could refuse him as a deliverer. But she would not tell him so, for her heart was still sore at his preference of Persis to herself.

Darius Hopkins had an uneasy visit at his aunt Tabitha's. He did not speak again of Persis Buckley, but he thought the more. Useless, as he told himself, as either hopes or fears were, they sprang up in his heart like persistent flames, and could not be trodden out.

He told himself that it was not sensible to think that the grand Englishman would ever come for Persis after all these years, and that it was nothing to him if he did. Yet he often trembled when he came in sight of her house lest he see a coach and four standing before it, and see her carried away before his very eyes.

And sometimes he would look at his own comely face in the glass, and look into his own heart, and feel as if the love therein must compel her even against her will; for she was not an angel or a goddess, after all, beautiful as she was, but only a mortal woman. "She cannot love this man whom she has not seen since she was a child, and he must be an old man now," reasoned

Darius, viewing his own gallant young face in the glass. And he smiled with hope, although he knew that he could not reasonably expect to have more of Persis than the sight of her face in the meeting-house or at the window were he to stay in the village a year.

For a long time Darius was not sure that Persis even noticed him when he passed by, but there came a day when he had that at least for his comfort. That day he had not passed her house until late ; on the day before her face had been so far turned from the window that his heart had sunk. He had said to himself that he would be such a love-cracked fool no longer ; he would not pass her house again unless of a necessity. So all that day he had sat moodily with his aunt, but just before dusk his resolution had failed him. He had strolled slowly across the meadow, while his aunt watched him from her window, smiling shrewdly.

He had not meant to glance even when he passed the Buckley house, but in spite of himself his eyes turned. And there was Persis at the window, leaning towards him, with her face all radiant with joy. It was only a second, and she was gone. Darius had no time for anything but that one look, but that was enough. He felt as if he had already routed the gallant with the coach and four. He meditated all sorts of audacious schemes as he went home. What could he not do, if Persis would only smile upon him ? He felt like marching straight upon her house, like a soldier upon a castle, and demanding her of her father, who was her jailer.

But the next day his heart failed him again, for she was not at her window—nor the next, nor the next. He could not know that she was peeping through the crack in the shutter, and that her embroidery and her reading and her old thoughts were all thrown aside for his sake. Persis Buckley could do nothing, day nor night, but think of Darius Hopkins, and watch for him to pass her window.

She did not know why, but she did not like to look fairly out of the window at him any longer. She could only peep through the crack in the shutter, with her color coming and going, and her heart beating loud in her ears.

But when Darius saw no more of Persis at the window, he told himself that his conceit had misled him ; that no such marvellous creature as that could have looked upon him as he had thought, and that his bold stare had affronted her.

So he did not pass the Buckley house for several days, and Persis watched in vain. One afternoon she rose up suddenly, with her soft cheek all creased where she had leaned it against the shutter. "He will not come ; I will watch no longer," she said to herself, half angrily.

And she got out her green silk pelisse and her bonnet, and prepared to walk abroad. She went through the kitchen, and her sister Submit stared up at her from the hearth, which she was washing.

"You have not got on your veil, Persis," said she.

"I want no veil," Persis returned, impatiently.

"But you will get burned in the wind; father will not like it," said Submit, with wondering and dull remonstrance.

"Well," sighed Persis, resignedly. And Submit got the black-wrought veil, and tied it over her sister's beautiful face.

Poor Persis, when she was out of the house, glanced hastily through the black maze of leaves and flowers across the meadow, but she saw no one coming. Then she strolled on away down the road through the woods. Just that side of the burying-ground there was an oak grove, and she went in there and sat down a little way from the road, with her back against a tree. It was very cool for the time of year, but the sun shone bright. All the oak-trees trilled sharply with the insects hidden in them, and the leaves rustled together.

Persis sat very stiffly under the oak-tree. Her petticoat was of green flowered chintz, and her pelisse and her bonnet of green silk. She was as undistinguishable as a green plant against the trunk of the tree, and neither Darius Hopkins nor his aunt Tabitha saw her when they passed. Persis heard their voices before they came in sight. She scarcely breathed. She seemed to be fairly hiding within herself, and forcing her very thoughts away from the eyes of Darius and his aunt.

Mistress Tabitha came down the wood, stepping with her fine mincing gait, and leaning upon her nephew's arm. They never dreamed that Persis was near. The green waving lines of the forest met their eyes on either hand, but all unnoted, being as it were the revolutions of that green wheel of nature of which long acquaintance had dimmed their perception. Only an unusual motion therein could arouse their attention when their thoughts were elsewhere, and they were talking busily.

As they came opposite Persis, Mistress Tabitha cried out suddenly, and her voice was full of dismay. "Not to-morrow!" she cried out. "You go not to-morrow, Darius!"

And Darius replied, sadly: "I must, Aunt Tabitha. I must go back to Boston by the Thursday stage-coach, and to-day is Wednesday."

Persis heard no more. She felt faint, and there was a strange singing in her ears. As soon as the aunt and nephew were well past, she got up and hastened back to the house. She took off her bonnet and pelisse, and sat down in her old place at the window, where she had watched so many years through her strange warped youth. When she saw Darius and his aunt returning, all her soul seemed to leap forward and look out of her great dark eyes. But Darius never glanced her way. He knew she was there, for his aunt said, "There is Persis Buckley," and nodded; but he dared not look, for fear lest he look too boldly, and she be offended.

Persis did not nod in response to Mistress Tabitha. She only looked, and looked at the slight, straight figure of the young man moving past her and out of her life. She thought that it was the last time that she should ever see him —the Boston stage left at daybreak. It seemed to her that he would never come again; and if he did, that she could not live until the time, but should ride away first from her old home forever, in gloomier state than had been planned for so many years.

When Darius and his aunt were out of sight she heard her father's voice in the kitchen, and she arose and went out there with a sudden resolve. "Father," she said, standing before Ichabod.

He looked at her in a curious startled way. There was a strange gleam in her soft eyes, and a strange expression about her docile mouth.

"What is it?" he said.

"He will never come, father. I want to be different."

"Who will never come? What do you mean, Persis?"

"The—gentleman—the grand gentleman with —the coach and four. He will never come for me now. I want to be different, father. I want to work with Submit, and not stay in there by myself. If I have to any longer I shall die, I think. I want to be different. He will never come now, father."

Ichabod Buckley trembled with long convulsive tremors, which seemed to leave him rigid and stiff as they passed. "He will come!" he returned, and he shouted out the words like an oath.

Submit, who was preparing supper, stopped, and stood pale and staring.

Persis quailed a little, but she spoke again.

"It is too long now, father," she said. "He has forgotten me. He has married another in England. He will never come, and I want to be different. And should he come, after all, I should be sorely afraid to go with him now. I could never go with him now, father."

Ichabod turned upon her, and spoke with such force that she shrank, as if before a stormy blast. "I tell ye he will come!" he shouted, hoarsely. "He will come, and you shall go with him, whether you will or no! He will come, and you shall sit there in that room and wait for him until he comes! You should wait there until you were dead, if he came not before. But he will, I tell ye—*he will come!*"

Persis fled before her father back to the best room, and sat there in the gathering dusk. Across the meadows the light of Tabitha Hopkins's evening candle shone out suddenly like a low-hung star, and Persis sat watching it. When Submit called, in a scared voice, that supper was ready, she went out at once, and took her place at the table. There were pink spots in her usually pale cheeks; she spoke not a word, and scarcely tasted the little tid-bits grouped as usual around her plate. Her father swallowed his food with nervous gulps, then he left the table and went out. Soon Persis heard the grate of his tools on the gravestone slate, and knew that he had gone to work by candle-light, something he seldom did.

"Father is put out," Submit said, with a half-scared, half-reproachful look at Persis.

"Oh, Submit!" Persis cried out, with the first appeal she had ever made in her life to her slow-witted elder sister, "I must be different, or I think I shall die!"

"Maybe he will come soon," said Submit, who did not understand her sister's appeal. "Maybe he will come soon, Persis. Father thinks so," she repeated, as she rose from the table and padded heavily about, removing the supper dishes.

Then she added something which filled her sister's soul with fright and dismay.

"Father he dreamt a dream last night," said Submit, in her thick drone. "He dreamt that the grand gentleman came with the coach and four, and the black gentleman a-driving, and the grand lady in a velvet hood, just as he came before, and you got in and rode away. And he dreamt he came on a Thursday."

"To-morrow is Thursday," gasped Persis.

Submit nodded. "Father thinks he will come to-morrow," said she. "He bade me not tell you, but I will for your comfort."

Submit stared wonderingly at her sister's distressed face as she ran out of the room; then she went on with her work. She presently, in sweeping the hearth, made a long black mark thereon, and straightway told herself that there was another sign that the gentleman was coming. Submit was well versed in New England domestic superstition, that being her only exercise of imagination.

Persis did not light the candles in the best room. She sat at the window in the dark, and watched again Mistress Tabitha's candle-light across the meadow. She also stared from time to time in a startled way in the other direction towards the woodland road. Persis also was superstitious. She feared lest her father's dream come true. She seemed to almost see now and then that stately equipage emerge as of old from the woods. She almost thought that she heard the far-away rumble of the wheels. She kept reminding herself that it was Wednesday, and her father's dream said Thursday; but what if she did have to go away forever with that strange gentleman only the next day! She thought suddenly, not knowing why, of Clarissa Harlowe and Lovelace in her book. Mistress Tabitha's purpose had not wholly failed in its effect. A great vague horror of something which she was too ignorant to see fairly came over her. The face of that fine strange gentleman, dimly remembered before through all the years, shaped itself suddenly and plainly out of the darkness like the face of a demon. Persis looked away, shuddering, to the candle-gleam over the meadow, and Darius Hopkins's eyes seemed to look wistfully and lovingly into hers.

Persis Buckley arose softly, groped her way across the room in the dark, sliding noiselessly like a shadow, felt for the latch of the door that led into the front entry, lifted it cautiously, stole out into the entry, then opened the outer door with careful pains by degrees, and was out of the house.

Persis fled then past the plumy gloom of the pine-trees that skirted the wood, over the meadow, straight towards that candle-gleam in the Hopkins window.

There was a dry northeaster blowing, and it struck her as she fled, and lashed her clothing about her. She had on no outer wraps, and her head and her delicate face, which had always been veiled before a zephyr, were now all roughened and buffeted by this strong wind, which carried the sting of salt in it.

She never thought of it nor minded it. She fled on and on like a love-compelled bird, with only one single impulse in her whole being. The measure of freedom is always in proportion to the measure of previous restraint. Persis Buckley had been under a restraint which no maiden in this New England village had ever suffered, and she had gotten from it an impetus for a deed which they would have blushed to think of.

She fled on, forcing her way against the wind, which sometimes seemed to meet her like a moving wall, and sometimes like the rushing legions of that Prince of the Powers of the Air of whom she had read in the Bible, making as if they would lift her up bodily and carry her away among them into unknown tumult and darkness.

When Persis reached Tabitha Hopkins's door, she was nearly spent. Her life had not trained her well for a flight in the teeth of the wind.

She leaned against the door for a minute faint and gasping.

Then she raised the knocker, and it fell with only a slight clang; but directly she heard an inner door open, and a step.

Then the door swung back before her, and Darius Hopkins stood there in the dim candle-light shining from the room within.

He could not see Persis's face plainly at first, only her little white hands reaching out to him like a child's from the gloom.

"Who is it?" he asked, doubtfully, and his voice trembled.

Persis made a little panting sound that was half a sob. Darius bent forward, peering out. Then he cried out, and caught at those little beseeching hands.

"It is not you!" he cried. "It is not you! You have not come to me! It is not you!"

Darius Hopkins, scarcely knowing what he did, he was so stirred with joy and triumph and doubt and fear, led Persis into the house and the candle-lit room. Then, when he saw in truth before him that beautiful face which he had worshipped from afar, the young man trembled and fell down upon his knees before Persis as if she were indeed a queen, or an angel who had come to bless him, and kissed her hand.

But Persis stood there, trembling and pale, before him, with the tears falling from her wonderful eyes, and her sweet mouth quivering. "Do not let him carry me away," she pleaded, faintly.

Then Darius sprang to his feet and put his arms around her. " Who is it would carry you away ?" he said, angrily and tenderly. "No one shall have you. Who is it ?"

" The — gentleman — from over-seas," whispered Persis. Her soft wet cheek was pressed against Darius's.

"He has not come ?" he questioned, starting fiercely.

" No ; but—father has dreamed that he will —to-morrow."

Then Darius laughed gayly. " Dreams go by contraries," he said.

" Do not let him carry me away," Persis pleaded again, and she sobbed on his shoulder, and clung to him.

Darius held her more closely. " He shall never carry you away, even if he comes, against your will," he said. " Do not fear."

"I will go with nobody but you," whispered Persis in his ear.

And he trembled, scarcely believing that he heard aright. And, indeed, he scarcely believed even yet that he was not dreaming, and that he held this beautiful creature in his arms, and, more than all, that she had come to him of her own accord.

"You—do—not—mean— You cannot—oh, you cannot mean— You are an angel. There is no one like you. You cannot—you cannot feel so about me?" he whispered, brokenly, at length.

Persis nodded against his breast.

"And—that was why—you came?"

Persis nodded again.

Darius bent her head back until he could see her beautiful, tearful face. He gazed at it with reverent wonder, then he kissed her forehead, and gently loosed her arm from his neck, and led her over to a chair.

He knelt down before her then as if she were a queen upon a throne, and held her hands softly. Then he questioned her as to how she had come, and about the expected coming of her strange gentleman suitor, and she answered him like a docile child.

Mistress Tabitha Hopkins stood for quite a time in the doorway, and neither of them saw her. Then she spoke up.

"I want to know what this means," said she. "How came she here?" She pointed a sharp forefinger at Persis, who shrank before it.

But Darius arose quickly and went forward, blushing, but full of manly confidence. "Come out with me a moment, Aunt Tabitha," he said; "I have something to say to you privately." He took his aunt's arm and led her out of the room, and, as he went, smiled back at Persis. "Do not be afraid, sweetheart," he said.

"Sweetheart!" sniffed Mistress Tabitha, before the door closed.

Persis Buckley had been gone no longer than an hour from her own home when Darius and his aunt Tabitha escorted her back. She was wrapped then in a warm cloak of Mistress Tabitha's, and clung to her lover's arm, and he leaned between her and the rough wind, and sheltered her. Poor Mistress Tabitha, with her skirts whipping about her and her ears full of wind, forced often by the onset of the gale at her back into staggering runs, pressed along after them. She had declined with some asperity her nephew's proffered assistance. "You look out for her," she said, shortly. And then she added, to temper her refusal, that she could better keep her cloak around her if both her arms were free. All her life had Mistress Tabitha Hopkins seen love only from the outside, shining in her neighbor's window. It was to her credit tonight if she was not all bitter when its light fell on her solitary old maiden face, but got a certain reflected warmth and joy from it.

Nobody had missed Persis. Submit was fairly knitting in her sleep, by the kitchen fire. Ichabod was still out in his shed at work.

Mistress Tabitha stood back a little while her nephew bade Persis good-bye at her door. "Remember, do not be frightened, whatever happens to-morrow," he whispered in her ear. "If the gentleman comes with the coach and four, go with him, and trust in me."

"I will do whatever you bid me," whispered Persis. Then Darius kissed her hand, and she stole softly through the dark doorway into the gloom of the house, while her faith in her lover was as a lamp to all her thoughts.

On the next afternoon there was a sensation in this little seaport town. A grand coach and four, with a black man driving, a fine gentleman's head at one window, and a fine lady's at another, came dashing through the place at two o'clock. The women all ran to the doors and windows. Lounging old men straightened themselves languidly to stare, and turned their vacant faces over their shoulders. A multitude of small lads, with here and there a little petticoat among them, collected rapidly, and pelted along in the wake of this grand equipage. They followed it quite through the town to the road that led through the woods, past the graveyard, to the Buckley house, then up the road, panting but eager, the smaller children dragging at the hands of their elder brothers. When they reached the Buckley house, this small rabble separated itself into decorously silent, primly courtesying rows on either side of the way. Then the grand coach and four at length turned about, and moved between the courtesying rows of children, while Ichabod Buckley stood proudly erect in his best green surtout watching it, and poor Submit, with a scrubbing-cloth in her hand, peeped around the house corner, and the Buckley Lady rode away.

And all the people saw the coach and four dash at a rattling pace back through the town, with the Buckley Lady's face set like a white lily in a window, and her grand suitor's fair head opposite. They also saw another lady beside Persis; her face was well hidden in her great velvet hood and wrought veil, but she sat up with a stately air.

The children followed the coach on the Boston road as far as they were able, then they straggled homeward, and the coach went out of sight in a great billow of dust.

It was several days before the people knew what had really happened — that Persis Buckley had gone away with Darius Hopkins, with a fair wig over his black hair, and the fine lady in the velvet hood had been nobody but Mistress Tabitha.

Darius Hopkins had sent a letter to the parson, and begged him to acquaint Ichabod Buckley with the truth, and humbly to crave his pardon for himself and Persis, who was now his wife, for the deceit they had practised. "But, in truth," wrote Darius Hopkins, "my beloved

wife was not acquaint with the plan at all, it
being contrived by my aunt, who hath a shrewd
head, and carried out by myself; and I doubt
much if she fairly knew with whom she went at
the very first, being quite overcome by her fright
and bewilderment." And Darius Hopkins begged
the parson also to acquaint Ichabod Buckley,
for his comfort, with this fact: Although his
daughter Persis had not wedded with a gentleman of high estate from over-seas, yet he, Darius
Hopkins, was of no mean birth, and had a not
inconsiderable share of this world's goods, with
more in expectation, as his esteemed aunt bade
him mention. And furthermore, Darius Hopkins stated that had he believed any other way
than the one he had taken to be available for the
purpose of winning his beloved wife and free-
ing her from a hard and unhappy lot, he would
much have preferred it. But he had taken this,
believing there was no other, in all honesty and
purity of purpose, and he again humbly begged
Ichabod Buckley's pardon.

One afternoon the parson paced solemnly up
to the Buckley house with the great red-sealed
letter in his hand. Ichabod was not at work.
His nervous old face was visible at the window
where his daughter's beautiful one had been so
long, and the parson went in the front door.

It was two hours before he came out, and went
with his head bent gravely down the road. He

never told exactly what had passed between himself and Ichabod Buckley, but it was whispered that the parson had striven in prayer for him for the space of an hour and a half, but had not reconciled him to his disappointment.

After his daughter had departed in state, Ichabod Buckley, while not returning to his old garrulous ways, but comporting himself with a dignity that would have befitted a squire, was seen frequently in the store and on the street, and he wore always his best green surtout, which he had heretofore kept for Sabbath days.

But after the truth was revealed to him Ichabod Buckley was seen no more abroad. He shut himself up in his poor workshed, and all day long his chisel rasped on the dark slate. Persis wrote to him, and Darius, and he read the letters, scowling fiercely and painfully through his iron-bowed spectacles, then put them away in his beetling old desk in the kitchen, and fell to work again.

It was not three weeks after Persis went away when Submit, with her apron over her head, went one morning through the woods with lumbering swiftness and called the doctor, for her father lay on his bed as motionless as if he were dead, and could not speak.

They sent for Persis, but her father was dead before she reached her old home and went weeping over the threshold, leaning on her young husband's arm. Not a word did she have of blame or forgiveness from her father's lips; but she knew his last mind towards her when she saw what his work had been since the day she left him.

Out in Ichabod Buckley's workshop stood a tall slate stone, shaped like the one he had erected for his dearly beloved wife. On it were cut his name, and the years of his birth and death, and under that a verse. In his own poor brain, strained almost asunder with its awful stress of one idea in life, he had devised this verse; with his poor old failing hands he had cut it on the stone:

"Stranger, view well this speaking stone,
 And drop a pitying tear;
Ingratitude had overthrown,
 And Death then laid me here."

Ichabod Buckley had left a space below, as if he had designed to make still larger his appeal to the pity of those who should pause in the future by his grave; and thereon did Darius Hopkins, to comfort his wife Persis, who grieved as if she could never be comforted when she read the first, cut another verse.

When the stone was set up over Ichabod's grave, people kneeling before it read, after the piteous complaint and prayer for sympathy of the dead man, Darius's verse:

"Who doth his clearer sight possess
In brighter realms above,
May come his earthly woe to bless,
And know that all was Love."

And it has so happened, because Darius cut
with his strong young hands more firmly and
deeply his verse in the stone, that his has en-
dured and can be read, while Ichabod's is all
worn away by the rain-storms of the years, as it
might have been by the tears of mortal life.

EVELINA'S GARDEN

O<small>N</small> the south a high arbor-vitæ hedge separated Evelina's garden from the road. The
hedge was so high that when the school-children
lagged by, and the secrets behind it fired them
with more curiosity than those between their
battered book covers, the tallest of them by
stretching up on tiptoe could not peer over.
And so they were driven to childish engineering
feats, and would set to work and pick away sprigs
of the arbor-vitæ with their little fingers, and
make peep-holes—but small ones, that Evelina
might not discern them. Then they would
thrust their pink faces into the hedge, and the
enduring fragrance of it would come to their
nostrils like a gust of aromatic breath from the
mouth of the northern woods, and peer into
Evelina's garden as through the green tubes of
vernal telescopes.

Then suddenly hollyhocks, blooming in rank
and file, seemed to be marching upon them like
platoons of soldiers, with detonations of color

111

that dazzled their peeping eyes; and, indeed, the whole garden seemed charging with its mass of riotous bloom upon the hedge. They could scarcely take in details of marigold and phlox and pinks and London-pride and cock's-combs, and prince's-feathers waving overhead like standards.

Sometimes also there was the purple flutter of Evelina's gown; and Evelina's face, delicately faded, hung about with softly drooping gray curls, appeared suddenly among the flowers, like another flower uncannily instinct with nervous melancholy.

Then the children would fall back from their peep-holes, and huddle off together with scared giggles. They were afraid of Evelina. There was a shade of mystery about her which stimulated their childish fancies when they heard her discussed by their elders. They might easily have conceived her to be some baleful fairy intrenched in her green stronghold, withheld from leaving it by the fear of some dire penalty for magical sins. Summer and winter, spring and fall, Evelina Adams never was seen outside her own domain of old mansion-house and garden, and she had not set her slim lady feet in the public highway for nearly forty years, if the stories were true.

People differed as to the reason why. Some said she had had an unfortunate love affair, that

her heart had been broken, and she had taken
upon herself a vow of seclusion from the world,
but nobody could point to the unworthy lover
who had done her this harm. When Evelina was
a girl, not one of the young men of the village
had dared address her. She had been set apart
by birth and training, and also by a certain exclusiveness of manner, if not of nature. Her
father, old Squire Adams, had been the one man
of wealth and college learning in the village. He
had owned the one fine old mansion-house, with
its white front propped on great Corinthian pillars, overlooking the village like a broad brow of
superiority.

He had owned the only coach and four. His
wife during her short life had gone dressed in
rich brocades and satins that rustled loud in the
ears of the village women, and her nodding
plumes had dazzled the eyes under their modest
hoods. Hardly a woman in the village but could
tell—for it had been handed down like a folk-lore
song from mother to daughter—just what Squire
Adams's wife wore when she walked out first as
bride to meeting. She had been clad all in blue.

"Squire Adams's wife, when she walked out
bride, she wore a blue satin brocade gown, all
wrought with blue flowers of a darker blue, cut
low neck and short sleeves. She wore long blue
silk mitts wrought with blue, blue satin shoes,
and blue silk clocked stockings. And she wore

a blue crape mantle that was brought from over-
seas, and a blue velvet hat, with a long blue os-
trich feather curled over it—it was so long it
reached her shoulder, and waved when she walked;
and she carried a little blue crape fan with ivory
sticks." So the women and girls told each other
when the Squire's bride had been dead nearly
seventy years.

The blue bride attire was said to be still in existence, packed away in a cedar chest, as the
Squire had ordered after his wife's death. " He
stood over the woman that took care of his wife
whilst she packed the things away, and he never
shed a tear, but she used to hear him a-goin' up
to the north chamber nights, when he couldn't
sleep, to look at 'em," the women told.

People had thought the Squire would marry
again. They said Evelina, who was only four
years old, needed a mother, and they selected one
and another of the good village girls. But the
Squire never married. He had a single woman,
who dressed in black silk, and wore always a black
wrought veil over the side of her bonnet, come
to live with them, to take charge of Evelina. She
was said to be a distant relative of the Squire's
wife, and was much looked up to by the village
people, although she never did more than inter-
lace, as it were, the fringes of her garments with
theirs. "She's stuck up," they said, and felt,
curiously enough, a certain pride in the fact when

they met her in the street and she ducked her
long chin stiffly into the folds of her black shawl
by way of salutation.

When Evelina was fifteen years old this single
woman died, and the village women went to her
funeral, and bent over her lying in a last helpless dignity in her coffin, and stared with awed
freedom at her cold face. After that Evelina
was sent away to school, and did not return, except for a yearly vacation, for six years to come.
Then she returned, and settled down in her old
home to live out her life, and end her days in a
perfect semblance of peace, if it were not peace.

Evelina never had any young school friend to
visit her; she had never, so far as any one knew,
a friend of her own age. She lived alone with
her father and three old servants. She went to
meeting, and drove with the Squire in his chaise.
The coach was never used after his wife's death,
except to carry Evelina to and from school. She
and the Squire also took long walks, but they
never exchanged aught but the merest civilities
of good-days and nods with the neighbors whom
they met, unless indeed the Squire had some
matter of business to discuss. Then Evelina
stood aside and waited, her fair face drooping
gravely aloof. She was very pretty, with a gentle
high-bred prettiness that impressed the village
folk, although they looked at it somewhat
askance.

Evelina's figure was tall, and had a fine slenderness ; her silken skirts hung straight from the narrow silk ribbon that girt her slim waist ; there was a languidly graceful bend in her long white throat ; her long delicate hands hung inertly at her sides among her skirt folds, and were never seen to clasp anything ; her softly clustering fair curls hung over her thin blooming cheeks, and her face could scarce be seen, unless, as she seldom did, she turned and looked full upon one. Then her dark blue eyes, with a little nervous frown between them, shone out radiantly ; her thin lips showed a warm red, and her beauty startled one.

Everybody wondered why she did not have a lover, why some fine young man had not been smitten by her while she had been away at school. They did not know that the school had been situated in another little village, the counterpart of the one in which she had been born, wherein a fitting mate for a bird of her feather could hardly be found. The simple young men of the country-side were at once attracted and intimidated by her. They cast fond sly glances across the meeting-house at her lovely face, but they were confused before her when they jostled her in the doorway and the rose and lavender scent of her lady garments came in their faces. Not one of them dared accost her, much less march boldly upon the great Corinthian-pillared house, raise

the brass knocker, and declare himself a suitor
for the Squire's daughter.

One young man there was. indeed, who treas-
ured in his heart an experience so subtle and so
slight that he could scarcely believe in it himself.
He never recounted it to mortal soul, but kept it
as a secret sacred between himself and his own
nature, but something to be scoffed at and set
aside by others.

It had happened one Sabbath day in summer,
when Evelina had not been many years home from
school, as she sat in the meeting-house in her
Sabbath array of rose-colored satin gown, and
white bonnet trimmed with a long white feather
and a little wreath of feathery green, that of a
sudden she raised her head and turned her face,
and her blue eyes met this young man's full upon
hers, with all his heart in them, and it was for a
second as if her own heart leaped to the surface,
and he saw it, although afterwards he scarce believed it to be true.

Then a pallor crept over Evelina's delicately
brilliant face. She turned it away, and her curls
falling softly from under the green wreath on
her bonnet brim hid it. The young man's cheeks
were a hot red, and his heart beat loudly in his
ears when he met her in the doorway after the
sermon was done. His eager, timorous eyes
sought her face, but she never looked his way.
She laid her slim hand in its cream-colored silk

mitt on the Squire's arm ; her satin gown rustled
softly as she passed before him, shrinking against
the wall to give her room, and a faint fragrance
which seemed like the very breath of the unknown
delicacy and exclusiveness of life came to his bewildered senses.

Many a time he cast furtive glances across the
meeting-house at Evelina, but she never looked
his way again. If his timid boy-eyes could have
seen her cheek behind its veil of curls, he might
have discovered that the color came and went before his glances, although it was strange how she
could have been conscious of them ; but he never
knew.

And he also never knew how, when he walked
past the Squire's house of a Sunday evening,
dressed in his best, with his shoulders thrust con-
sciously back, and the windows in the westering
sun looked full of blank gold to his furtive eyes,
Evelina was always peeping at him from behind
a shutter, and he never dared go in. His intui-
tions were not like hers, and so nothing happened
that might have, and he never fairly knew what
he knew. But that he never told, even to his
wife when he married ; for his hot young blood
grew weary and impatient with this vain court-
ship, and he turned to one of his villagemates,
who met him fairly half way, and married her
within a year.

On the Sunday when he and his bride first ap-

peared in the meeting-house Evelina went up the
aisle behind her father in an array of flowered
brocade, stiff with threads of silver, so wonderful that people all turned their heads to stare at
her. She wore also a new bonnet of rose-colored
satin, and her curls were caught back a little, and
her face showed as clear and beautiful as an
angel's.

The young bridegroom glanced at her once
across the meeting-house, then he looked at his
bride in her gay wedding finery with a faithful
look.

When Evelina met them in the doorway, after
meeting was done, she bowed with a sweet cold
grace to the bride, who courtesied blushingly in
return, with an awkward sweep of her foot in the
bridal satin shoe. The bridegroom did not look
at Evelina at all. He held his chin well down in
his stock with solemn embarrassment, and passed
out stiffly, his bride on his arm.

Evelina, shining in the sun like a silver lily,
went up the street, her father stalking beside
her with stately swings of his cane, and that was
the last time she was ever seen at meeting. Nobody knew why.

When Evelina was a little over thirty her father
died. There was not much active grief for him
in the village; he had really figured therein more
as a stately monument of his own grandeur than
anything else. He had been a man of little force

of character, and that little had seemed to degenerate since his wife died. An inborn dignity of manner might have served to disguise his weakness with any others than these shrewd New-Englanders, but they read him rightly. "The Squire wa'n't ever one to set the river a-fire," they said. Then, moreover, he left none of his property to the village to build a new meeting-house or a town-house. It all went to Evelina.

People expected that Evelina would surely show herself in her mourning at meeting the Sunday after the Squire died, but she did not. Moreover, it began to be gradually discovered that she never went out in the village street nor crossed the boundaries of her own domains after her father's death. She lived in the great house with her three servants—a man and his wife, and the woman who had been with her mother when she died. Then it was that Evelina's garden began. There had always been a garden at the back of the Squire's house, but not like this, and only a low fence had separated it from the road. Now one morning in the autumn the people saw Evelina's man-servant, John Darby, setting out the arbor-vitæ hedge, and in the spring after that there were ploughing and seed-sowing extending over a full half-acre, which later blossomed out in glory.

Before the hedge grew so high Evelina could be seen at work in her garden. She was often stooping over the flower-beds in the early morning when the village was first astir, and she moved among them with her watering-pot in the twilight —a shadowy figure that might, from her grace and her constancy to the flowers, have been Flora herself.

As the years went on, the arbor-vitæ hedge got each season a new growth and waxed taller, until Evelina could no longer be seen above it. That was an annoyance to people, because the quiet mystery of her life kept their curiosity alive, until it was in a constant struggle, as it were, with the green luxuriance of the hedge.

"John Darby had ought to trim that hedge," they said. They accosted him in the street: "John, if ye don't cut that hedge down a little it 'll all die out." But he only made a surly grunting response, intelligible to himself alone, and passed on. He was an Englishman, and had lived in the Squire's family since he was a boy.

He had a nature capable of only one simple line of force, with no radiations or parallels, and that had early resolved itself into the service of the Squire and his house. After the Squire's death he married a woman who lived in the family. She was much older than himself, and had a high temper, but was a good servant, and he married her to keep her to her allegiance to Evelina. Then he bent her, without her knowledge, to take his own attitude towards his mistress. No more could be gotten out of John Darby's wife than out of John Darby concerning the doings at the Squire's house. She met curiosity with a flash of hot temper, and he with surly taciturnity, and both intimidated.

The third of Evelina's servants was the woman who had nursed her mother, and she was naturally subdued and undemonstrative, and rendered still more so by a ceaseless monotony of life. She never went to meeting, and was seldom seen outside the house. A passing vision of a long white-capped face at a window was about all the neighbors ever saw of this woman.

So Evelina's gentle privacy was well guarded by her own household, as by a faithful system of domestic police. She grew old peacefully behind her green hedge, shielded effectually from all rough bristles of curiosity. Every new spring her own bloom showed paler beside the new bloom of her flowers, but people could not see it.

Some thirty years after the Squire's death the man John Darby died; his wife, a year later. That left Evelina alone with the old woman who had nursed her mother. She was very old, but not feeble, and quite able to perform the simple household tasks for herself and Evelina. An old man, who saved himself from the almshouse in such ways, came daily to do the rougher part of the garden-work in John Darby's stead. He was aged and decrepit; his muscles seemed able to perform their appointed tasks only through the accumulated inertia of a patiently toilsome life in the same tracks. Apparently they would have collapsed had he tried to force them to aught else than the holding of the ploughshare, the pulling of weeds, the digging around the roots of flowers, and the planting of seeds.

Every autumn he seemed about to totter to his fall among the fading flowers; every spring it was like Death himself urging on the resurrection; but he lived on year after year, and tended well Evelina's garden, and the gardens of other maiden-women and widows in the village. He was taciturn, grubbing among his green beds as silently as a worm, but now and then he warmed a little under a fire of questions concerning Evelina's garden. "Never see none sech flowers in nobody's garden in this town, not sence I knowed 'nough to tell a pink from a piny," he would mumble. His speech was thick; his words were all uncouthly slurred; the expression of his whole life had come more through his old knotted hands of labor than through his tongue. But he would wipe his forehead with his shirt-sleeve and lean a second on his spade, and his face would change at the mention of the garden. Its wealth of bloom illumined his old mind, and the roses and honeysuckles and pinks seemed for a second to be reflected in his bleared old eyes.

There had never been in the village such a

garden as this of Evelina Adams's. All the old blooms which had come over the seas with the early colonists, and started as it were their own colony of flora in the new country, flourished there. The naturalized pinks and phlox and hollyhocks and the rest, changed a little in color and fragrance by the conditions of a new climate and soil, were all in Evelina's garden, and no one dreamed what they meant to Evelina; and she did not dream herself, for her heart was always veiled to her own eyes, like the face of a nun. The roses and pinks, the poppies and heart's-ease, were to this maiden-woman, who had innocently and helplessly outgrown her maiden heart, in the place of all the loves of life which she had missed. Her affections had forced an outlet in roses; they exhaled sweetness in pinks, and twined and clung in honeysuckle-vines. The daffodils, when they came up in the spring, comforted her like the smiles of children; when she saw the first rose, her heart leaped as at the face of a lover.

She had lost the one way of human affection, but her feet had found a little single side-track of love, which gave her still a zest in the journey of life. Even in the winter Evelina had her flowers, for she kept those that would bear transplanting in pots, and all the sunny windows in her house were gay with them. She would also not let a rose leaf fall and waste in the garden soil, or a sprig of lavender or thyme. She gathered them all, and stored them away in chests and drawers and old china bowls—the whole house seemed laid away in rose leaves and lavender. Evelina's clothes gave out at every motion that fragrance of dead flowers which is like the fragrance of the past, and has a sweetness like that of sweet memories. Even the cedar chest where Evelina's mother's blue bridal array was stored had its till heaped with rose leaves and lavender.

When Evelina was nearly seventy years old the old nurse who had lived with her her whole life died. People wondered then what she would do. "She can't live all alone in that great house," they said. But she did live there alone six months, until spring, and people used to watch her evening lamp when it was put out, and the morning smoke from her kitchen chimney. "It ain't safe for her to be there alone in that great house," they said.

But early in April a young girl appeared one Sunday in the old Squire's pew. Nobody had seen her come to town, and nobody knew who she was or where she came from, but the old people said she looked just as Evelina Adams used to when she was young, and she must be some relation. The old man who had used to look across the meeting-house at Evelina, over forty years ago, looked across now at this young girl, and gave a great start, and his face paled under his gray beard stubble. His old wife gave an

anxious, wondering glance at him, and crammed
a peppermint into his hand. "Anything the
matter, father?" she whispered; but he only
gave his head a half-surly shake, and then fastened his eyes straight ahead upon the pulpit.
He had reason to that day, for his only son,
Thomas, was going to preach his first sermon
therein as a candidate. His wife ascribed his
nervousness to that. She put a peppermint in
her own mouth and sucked it comfortably.
"That's all 'tis," she thought to herself. "Father always was easy worked up," and she looked
proudly up at her son sitting on the hair-cloth
sofa in the pulpit, leaning his handsome young
head on his hand, as he had seen old divines do.
She never dreamed that her old husband sitting
beside her was possessed of an inner life so strange
to her that she would not have known him had
she met him in the spirit. And, indeed, it had
been so always, and she had never dreamed of it.
Although he had been faithful to his wife, the
image of Evelina Adams in her youth, and that
one love-look which she had given him, had
never left his soul, but had given it a guise and
complexion of which his nearest and dearest knew
nothing.

It was strange; but now, as he looked up at his
own son as he arose in the pulpit, he could seem
to see a look of that fair young Evelina, who had
never had a son to inherit her beauty. He had

certainly a delicate brilliancy of complexion, which he could have gotten directly from neither father nor mother; and whence came that little nervous frown between his dark blue eyes? His mother had blue eyes, but not like his; they flashed over the great pulpit Bible with a sweet fire that matched the memory in his father's heart.

But the old man put the fancy away from him in a minute; it was one which his stern common-sense always overcame. It was impossible that Thomas Merriam should resemble Evelina Adams; indeed, people always called him the very image of his father.

The father tried to fix his mind upon his son's sermon, but presently he glanced involuntarily across the meeting-house at the young girl, and again his heart leaped and his face paled; but he turned his eyes gravely back to the pulpit, and his wife did not notice. Now and then she thrust a sharp elbow in his side to call his attention to a grand point in their son's discourse. The odor of peppermint was strong in his nostrils, but through it all he seemed to perceive the rose and lavender scent of Evelina Adams's youthful garments. Whether it was with him simply the memory of an odor, which affected him like the odor itself, or not, those in the vicinity of the Squire's pew were plainly aware of it. The gown which the strange young girl wore was, as many an old woman discovered to her neighbor with loud whispers, one of Evelina's, which had been laid away in a sweet-smelling chest since her old girlhood. It had been somewhat altered to suit the fashion of a later day, but the eyes which had fastened keenly upon it when Evelina first wore it up the meeting-house aisle could not mistake it. "It's Evelina Adams's lavender satin made over," one whispered, with a sharp hiss of breath, in the other's ear.

The lavender satin, deepening into purple in the folds, swept in a rich circle over the knees of the young girl in the Squire's pew. She folded her little hands, which were encased in Evelina's cream-colored silk mitts, over it, and looked up at the young minister, and listened to his sermon with a grave and innocent dignity, as Evelina had done before her. Perhaps the resemblance between this young girl and the young girl of the past was more one of mien than aught else, although the type of face was the same. This girl had the same fine sharpness of feature and delicately bright color, and she also wore her hair in curls, although they were tied back from her face with a black velvet ribbon, and did not veil it when she drooped her head, as Evelina's used to do.

The people divided their attention between her and the new minister. Their curiosity goaded them in equal measure with their spiritual zeal.

"I can't wait to find out who that girl is," one woman whispered to another.

The girl herself had no thought of the commotion which she awakened. When the service was over, and she walked with a gentle maiden stateliness, which seemed a very copy of Evelina's own, out of the meeting-house, down the street to the Squire's house, and entered it, passing under the stately Corinthian pillars, with a last purple gleam of her satin skirts, she never dreamed of the eager attention that followed her.

It was several days before the village people discovered who she was. The information had to be obtained, by a process like mental thumb-screwing, from the old man who tended Evelina's garden, but at last they knew. She was the daughter of a cousin of Evelina's on the father's side. Her name was Evelina Leonard; she had been named for her father's cousin. She had been finely brought up, and had attended a Boston school for young ladies. Her mother had been dead many years, and her father had died some two years ago, leaving her with only a very little money, which was now all gone, and Evelina Adams had invited her to live with her. Evelina Adams had herself told the old gardener, seeing his scant curiosity was somewhat awakened by the sight of the strange young lady in the garden, but he seemed to have almost forgotten it when the people questioned him.

"She'll leave her all her money, most likely," they said, and they looked at this new Evelina in the old Evelina's perfumed gowns with awe.

However, in the space of a few months the opinion upon this matter was divided. Another cousin of Evelina Adams's came to town, and this time an own cousin—a widow in fine black bombazine, portly and florid, walking with a majestic swell, and, moreover, having with her two daughters, girls of her own type, not so far advanced. This woman hired one of the village cottages, and it was rumored that Evelina Adams paid the rent. Still, it was considered that she was not very intimate with these last relatives. The neighbors watched, and saw, many a time, Mrs. Martha Loomis and her girls try the doors of the Adams house, scudding around angrily from front, to side and back, and knock and knock again, but with no admittance. "Evelina she won't let none of 'em in more'n once a week," the neighbors said. It was odd that, although they had deeply resented Evelina's seclusion on their own accounts, they were rather on her side in this matter, and felt a certain delight when they witnessed a crestfallen retreat of the widow and her daughters. "I don't s'pose she wants them Loomises marchin' in on her every minute," they said.

The new Evelina was not seen much with the other cousins, and she made no acquaintances in

the village. Whether she was to inherit all the
Adams property or not, she seemed, at any rate,
heiress to all the elder Evelina's habits of life.
She worked with her in the garden, and wore her
old girlish gowns, and kept almost as close at
home as she. She often, however, walked abroad
in the early dusk, stepping along in a grave and
stately fashion, as the elder Evelina had used to
do, holding her skirts away from the dewy road-
side weeds, her face showing out in the twilight
like a white flower, as if it had a pale light of its
own.

Nobody spoke to her; people turned furtively
after she had passed and stared after her, but
they never spoke. This young Evelina did not
seem to expect it. She passed along with the
lids cast down over her blue eyes, and the rose
and lavender scent of her garments came back in
their faces.

But one night when she was walking slowly
along, a full half-mile from home, she heard
rapid footsteps behind, and the young minister,
Thomas Merriam, came up beside her and spoke.

"Good-evening," said he, and his voice was a
little hoarse through nervousness.

Evelina started, and turned her fair face up
towards his. "Good-evening," she responded,
and courtesied as she had been taught at school,
and stood close to the wall, that he might pass;
but Thomas Merriam paused also.

"I—" he began, but his voice broke. He cleared his throat angrily, and went on. "I have seen you in meeting," he said, with a kind of defiance, more of himself than of her. After all, was he not the minister, and had he not the right to speak to everybody in the congregation? Why should he embarrass himself?

"Yes, sir," replied Evelina. She stood drooping her head before him, and yet there was a certain delicate hauteur about her. Thomas was afraid to speak again. They both stood silent for a moment, and then Evelina stirred softly, as if to pass on, and Thomas spoke out bravely. "Is your cousin, Miss Adams, well?" said he.

"She is pretty well, I thank you, sir."

"I have been wanting to—call," he began; then he hesitated again. His handsome young face was blushing crimson.

Evelina's own color deepened. She turned her face away. "Cousin Evelina never sees callers," she said, with grave courtesy; "perhaps you did not know. She has not for a great many years."

"Yes, I did know it," returned Thomas Merriam; "that's the reason I haven't called."

"Cousin Evelina is not strong," remarked the young girl, and there was a savor of apology in her tone.

"But—" stammered Thomas; then he stopped again. "May I—has she any objections to—anybody's coming to see you?"

"SHE HEARD RAPID FOOTSTEPS"

Evelina started. "I am afraid Cousin Evelina would not approve," she answered, primly. Then she looked up in his face, and a girlish piteousness came into her own. "I am very sorry," she said, and there was a catch in her voice.

Thomas bent over her impetuously. All his ministerial state fell from him like an outer garment of the soul. He was young, and he had seen this girl Sunday after Sunday. He had written all his sermons with her image before his eyes, he had preached to her, and her only, and she had come between his heart and all the nations of the earth in his prayers. "Oh," he stammered out, "I am afraid you can't be very happy living there the way you do. Tell me—"

Evelina turned her face away with sudden haughtiness. "My cousin Evelina is very kind to me, sir," she said.

"But—you must be lonesome with nobody—of your own age—to speak to," persisted Thomas, confusedly.

"I never cared much for youthful company. It is getting dark; I must be going," said Evelina. "I wish you good-evening, sir."

"Sha'n't I — walk home with you?" asked Thomas, falteringly.

"It isn't necessary, thank you, and I don't think Cousin Evelina would approve," she replied, primly ; and her light dress fluttered away

into the dusk and out of sight like the pale wing
of a moth.

Poor Thomas Merriam walked on with his head
in a turmoil. His heart beat loud in his ears.
"I've made her mad with me," he said to himself, using the old rustic school-boy vernacu-
lar, from which he did not always depart in
his thoughts, although his ministerial dignity
guarded his conversations. Thomas Merriam
came of a simple homely stock, whose speech
came from the emotions of the heart, all unregu-
lated by the usages of the schools. He was the
first for generations who had aspired to college
learning and a profession, and had trained his
tongue by the models of the educated and polite.
He could not help, at times, the relapse of his
thoughts, and their speaking to himself in the
dialect of his family and his ancestors. "She's
'way above me, and I ought to ha' known it," he
further said, with the meekness of an humble
but fiercely independent race, which is meek to
itself alone. He would have maintained his
equality with his last breath to an opponent ; in
his heart of hearts he felt himself below the scion
of the one old gentle family of his native village.

This young Evelina, by the fine dignity which
had been born with her and not acquired by pre-
cept and example, by the sweetly formal diction
which seemed her native tongue, had filled him
with awe. Now, when he thought she was an-

gered with him, he felt beneath her lady-feet, his
nostrils choked with a spiritual dust of humilia-
tion.

He went forward blindly. The dusk had deepened ; from either side of the road, from the mysterious gloom of the bushes, came the twangs of
the katydids, like some coarse rustic quarrellers,
each striving for the last word in a dispute not
even dignified by excess of passion.

Suddenly somebody jostled him to his own side
of the path. "That you, Thomas? Where you
been ?" said a voice in his ear.

"That you, father ? Down to the post-office."

"Who was that you was talkin' with back
there ?"

"Miss Evelina Leonard."

"That girl that's stayin' there—to the old
Squire's ?"

"Yes." The son tried to move on, but his
father stood before him dumbly for a minute.
"I must be going, father. I've got to work on
my sermon," Thomas said, impatiently.

"Wait a minute," said his father. "I've got
something to say to ye, Thomas, an' this is as
good a time to say it as any. There ain't anybody 'round. I don't know as ye'll thank me for
it—but mother said the other day that she thought
you'd kind of an idea—she said you asked her if
she thought it would be anything out of the way
for you to go up to the Squire's to make a call.

Mother she thinks you can step in anywheres, but
I don't know. I know your book-learnin' and
your bein' a minister has set you up a good deal
higher than your mother and me and any of our
folks, and I feel as if you were good enough for
anybody, as far as that goes; but that ain't all.
Some folks have different startin'-points in this
world, and they see things different; and when
they do, it ain't much use tryin' to make them
walk alongside and see things alike. Their eyes
have got different cants, and they ain't able to
help it. Now this girl she's related to the old
Squire, and she's been brought up different, and
she started ahead, even if her father did lose all
his property. She 'ain't never eat in the kitchen,
nor been scart to set down in the parlor, and satin
and velvet, and silver spoons, and cream-pots
'ain't never looked anything out of the common
to her, and they always will to you. No matter
how many such things you may live to have,
they'll always get a little the better of ye. She'll
be 'way above 'em; and you won't, no matter
how hard you try. Some ideas can't never mix;
and when ideas can't mix, folks can't."

"I never said they could," returned Thomas,
shortly. "I can't stop to talk any longer, father.
I must go home."

"No, you wait a minute, Thomas. I'm goin'
to say out what I started to, and then I sha'n't
ever bring it up again. What I was comin' at

136

was this: I wanted to warn ye a little. You musn't set too much store by little things that you think mean consider'ble when they don't. Looks don't count for much, and I want you to remember it, and not be upset by 'em."

Thomas gave a great start, and colored high. "I'd like to know what you mean, father," he cried, sharply.

"Nothin'. I don't mean nothin', only I'm older 'n you, and it's come in my way to know some things, and it's fittin' you should profit by it. A young woman's looks at you don't count for much. I don't s'pose she knows why she gives 'em herself half the time; they ain't like us. It's best you should make up your mind to it; if you don't, you may find it out by the hardest. That's all. I ain't never goin' to bring this up again."

"I'd like to know what you mean, father." Thomas's voice shook with embarrassment and anger.

"I ain't goin' to say anything more about it," replied the old man. "Mary Ann Pease and Arabella Mann are both in the settin'-room with your mother. I thought I'd tell ye, in case ye didn't want to see 'em, and wanted to go to work on your sermon."

Thomas made an impatient ejaculation as he strode off. When he reached the large white house where he lived he skirted it carefully. The

chirping treble of girlish voices came from the
open sitting - room window, and he caught a
glimpse of a smooth brown head and a high shell
comb in front of the candle-light. The young
minister tiptoed in the back door and across the
kitchen to the back stairs. The sitting-room
door was open, and the candle-light streamed
out, and the treble voices rose high. Thomas,
advancing through the dusky kitchen with cau-
tious steps, encountered suddenly a chair in the
dark corner by the stairs, and just saved himself
from falling. There was a startled outcry from
the sitting-room, and his mother came running
into the kitchen with a candle.

"Who is it?" she demanded, valiantly. Then
she started and gasped as her son confronted her.
He shook a furious warning fist at the sitting-
room door and his mother, and edged towards
the stairs. She followed him close. "Hadn't
you better jest step in a minute?" she whispered.
"Them girls have been here an hour, and I know
they're waitin' to see you." Thomas shook his
head fiercely, and swung himself around the corner into the dark crook of the back stairs. His
mother thrust the candle into his hand. "Take
this, or you'll break your neck on them stairs,"
she whispered.

Thomas, stealing up the stairs like a cat, heard
one of the girls call to his mother—"Is it robbers, Mis' Merriam? Want us to come an' help

138

tackle 'em ?"—and he fairly shuddered; for Evelina's gentle-lady speech was still in his ears, and
this rude girlish call seemed to jar upon his sensibilities.

"The idea of any girl screeching out like that,"
he muttered. And if he had carried speech as
far as his thought, he would have added, "when
Evelina is a girl!"

He was so angry that he did not laugh when
he heard his mother answer back, in those con-
clusive tones of hers that were wont to silence all
argument: "It ain't anything. Don't be scared.
I'm coming right back." Mrs. Merriam scorned
subterfuges. She took always a silent stand in
a difficulty, and let people infer what they would.
When Mary Ann Pease inquired if it was the cat
that had made the noise, she asked if her mother
had finished her blue and white counterpane.

The two girls waited a half-hour longer, then
they went home. "What do you s'pose made
that noise out in the kitchen?" asked Arabella
Mann of Mary Ann Pease, the minute they were
out-of-doors.

"I don't know," replied Mary Ann Pease. She
was a broad-backed young girl, and looked like a
matron as she hurried along in the dusk.

"Well, I know what I think it was," said Arabella Mann, moving ahead with sharp jerks of
her little dark body.

"What?"

"It was him."

"You don't mean—"

"I think it was Thomas Merriam, and he was tryin' to get up the back stairs unbeknownst to anybody, and he run into something."

"What for?"

"Because he didn't want to see *us*."

"Now, Arabella Mann, I don't believe it! He's always real pleasant to me."

"Well, I do believe it, and I guess he'll know it when I set foot in that house again. I guess he'll find out I didn't go there to see him! He needn't feel so fine, if he is the minister; his folks ain't any better than mine, an' we've got 'nough sight handsomer furniture in our parlor."

"Did you see how the tallow had all run down over the candles?"

"Yes, I did. She gave that candle she carried out in the kitchen to him, too. Mother says she wasn't never any kind of a housekeeper."

"Hush! Arabella: here he is coming now."

But it was not Thomas; it was his father, advancing through the evening with his son's gait and carriage. When the two girls discovered that, one tittered out quite audibly, and they scuttled past. They were not rivals; they simply walked faithfully side by side in pursuit of the young minister, giving him as it were an impartial choice. There were even no heart-burnings between them; one always confided in the other

140

when she supposed herself to have found some slight favor in Thomas's sight; and, indeed, the young minister could scarcely bow to one upon the street unless she flew to the other with the news.

Thomas Merriam himself was aware of all this devotion on the part of the young women of his flock, and it filled him with a sort of angry shame. He could not have told why, but he despised himself for being the object of their attention more than he despised them. His heart sank at the idea of Evelina's discovering it. What would she think of him if she knew all those young women haunted his house and lagged after meeting on the chance of getting a word from him? Suppose she should see their eyes upon his face in meeting time, and decipher their half-unconscious boldness, as he had done against his will. Once Evelina had looked at him, even as the older Evelina had looked at his father, and all other looks of maidens seemed to him like profanations of that, even although he doubted afterwards that he had rightly interpreted it. Full it had seemed to him of that tender maiden surprise and wonder, of that love that knows not itself, and sees its own splendor for the first time in another's face, and flees at the sight. It had happened once when he was coming down the aisle after the sermon and Evelina had met him at the door of her pew. But she had turned her head quickly, and her soft curls flowed over her red cheek, and he doubted ever after if he had read the look aright. When he had gotten the courage to speak to her, and she had met him with the gentle coldness which she had learned of her lady aunt and her teacher in Boston, his doubt was strong upon him. The next Sunday he looked not her way at all. He even tried faithfully from day to day to drive her image from his mind with prayer and religious thoughts, but in spite of himself he would lapse into dreams about her, as if borne by a current of nature too strong to be resisted. And sometimes, upon being awakened from them, as he sat over his sermon with the ink drying on his quill, by the sudden outburst of treble voices in his mother's sitting-room below, the fancy would seize him that possibly these other young damsels took fond liberties with him in their dreams, as he with Evelina, and he resented it with a fierce maidenliness of spirit, although he was a man. The thought that possibly they, over their spinning or their quilting, had in their hearts the image of himself with fond words upon his lips and fond looks in his eyes, filled him with shame and rage, although he took the same liberty with the delicately haughty maiden Evelina.

But Thomas Merriam was not given to undue appreciation of his own fascination, as was proved by his ready discouragement in the case of Eve-

lina. He had the knowledge of his conquests
forced upon his understanding until he could no
longer evade it. Every day were offerings laid
upon his shrine, of pound-cakes and flaky pies,
and loaves of white bread, and cups of jelly,
whereby the culinary skill of his devotees might
be proved. Silken purses and beautiful socks
knitted with fancy stitches, and holy book-marks
for his Bible, and even a wonderful bedquilt, and
a fine linen shirt with hem-stitched bands, poured
in upon him. He burned with angry blushes
when his mother, smiling meaningly, passed
them over to him. "Put them away, mother; I
don't want them," he would growl out, in a distress that was half comic and half pathetic. He
would never taste of the tempting viands which
were brought to him. "How you act, Thomas!"
his mother would say. She was secretly elated
by these feminine libations upon the altar of her
son. They did not grate upon her sensibilities,
which were not delicate. She even tried to assist
two or three of the young women in their designs;
she would often praise them and their handiwork
to her son—and in this she was aided by an old
woman aunt of hers who lived with the family.
"Nancy Winslow is as handsome a girl as ever I
set eyes on, an' I never see any nicer sewin',"
Mrs. Merriam said, after the advent of the linen
shirt, and she held it up to the light admiringly.
"Jest look at that hem-stitchin'!" she said.

"I guess whoever made that shirt calkilated 'twould do for a weddin' one," said old Aunt Betty Green, and Thomas made an exclamation and went out of the room, tingling all over with shame and disgust.

"Thomas don't act nateral," said the old woman, glancing after him through her iron-bound spectacles.

"I dun'no' what's got into him," returned his mother.

"Mebbe they foller him up a leetle too close," said Aunt Betty. "I dun'no' as I should have ventured on a shirt when I was a gal. I made a satin vest once for Joshua, but that don't seem quite as p'inted as a shirt. It didn't scare Joshua, nohow. He asked me to have him the next week."

"Well, I dun'no'," said Mrs. Merriam again. "I kind of wish Thomas would settle on somebody, for I'm pestered most to death with 'em, an' I feel as if 'twas kind of mean takin' all these things into the house."

"They've 'bout kept ye in sweet cake, 'ain't they, lately?"

"Yes; but I don't feel as if it was jest right for us to eat it up, when 'twas brought for Thomas. But he won't touch it. I can't see as he has the least idee of any one of them. I don't believe Thomas has ever seen anybody he wanted for a wife."

"Well, he's got the pick of 'em, a-settin' their caps right in his face," said Aunt Betty.

Neither of them dreamed how the young man, sleeping and eating and living under the same roof, beloved of them since he entered the world, holding himself coldly aloof from this crowd of half-innocently, half-boldly ardent young women, had set up for himself his own divinity of love, before whom he consumed himself in vain worship. His father suspected, and that was all, and he never mentioned the matter again to his son.

After Thomas had spoken to Evelina the weeks went on, and they never exchanged another word, and their eyes never met. But they dwelt constantly within each other's thoughts, and were ever present to each other's spiritual vision. Always as the young minister bent over his sermon-paper, laboriously tracing out with sputtering quill his application of the articles of the ortho-dox faith, Evelina's blue eyes seemed to look out at him between the stern doctrines like the eyes of an angel. And he could not turn the pages of the Holy Writ unless he found some passage therein which to his mind treated directly of her, setting forth her graces like a prophecy. "The fairest among women," read Thomas Merriam, and nodded his head, while his heart leaped with the satisfied delight of all its fancies, at the image of his love's fair and gentle face. "Her price is far above rubies," read Thomas Merriam, and he nodded his head again, and saw Evelina shining as with gold and pearls, more precious than all the jewels of the earth. In spite of all his efforts, when Thomas Merriam studied the Scriptures in those days he was more nearly touched by those old human hearts which throbbed down to his through the ages, welding the memories of their old loves to his living one until they seemed to prove its eternity, than by the Messianic prophecies. Often he spent hours upon his knees, but arose with Evelina's face before his very soul in spite of all.

And as for Evelina, she tended the flowers in the elder Evelina's garden with her poor cousin, whose own love-dreams had been illustrated as it were by the pinks and lilies blooming around them when they had all gone out of her heart, and Thomas Merriam's half-bold, half-imploring eyes looked up at her out of every flower and stung her heart like bees. Poor young Evelina feared much lest she had offended Thomas, and yet her own maiden decorum had been offended by him, and she had offended it herself, and she was faint with shame and distress when she thought of it. How had she been so bold and shameless as to give him that look in the meeting-house ? and how had he been so cruel as to accost her afterwards ? She told herself she had done right for the maintenance of her own maiden dignity, and yet she feared lest she had angered him and hurt him. "Suppose he had been fretted by her coolness?" she thought, and then a great wave of tender pity went over her heart, and she would almost have spoken to him of her own accord. But then she would reflect how he continued to write such beautiful sermons, and prove so clearly and logically the tenets of the faith; and how could he do that with a mind in distress? Scarcely could she herself tend the flower-beds as she should, nor set her embroidery stitches finely and evenly, she was so ill at ease. It must be that Thomas had not given the matter an hour's worry, since he continued to do his work so faithfully and well. And then her own heart would be sorer than ever with the belief that his was happy and at rest, although she would chide herself for it.

And yet this young Evelina was a philosopher and an analyst of human nature in a small way, and she got some slight comfort out of a shrewd suspicion that the heart of a man might love and suffer on a somewhat different principle from the heart of a woman. "It may be," thought Evelina, sitting idle over her embroidery with far-away blue eyes, "that a man's heart can always turn a while from love to other things as weighty and serious, although he be just as fond, while a woman's heart is always fixed one way by loving, and cannot be turned unless it breaks. And it may be wise," thought young Evelina, "else how could the state be maintained and governed, battles for independence be fought, and even souls be saved, and the gospel carried to the heathen, if men could not turn from the concerns of their own hearts more easily than women? Women should be patient," thought Evelina, "and consider that if they suffer 'tis due to the lot which a wise Providence has given them." And yet tears welled up in her earnest blue eyes and fell over her fair cheeks and wet the embroidery—when the elder Evelina was not looking, as she seldom was. The elder Evelina was kind to her young cousin, but there were days when she seemed to dwell alone in her own thoughts, apart from the whole world, and she seldom spoke either to Evelina or her old servant-man.

Young Evelina, trying to atone for her former indiscretion and establish herself again on her height of maiden reserve in Thomas Merriam's eyes, sat resolutely in the meeting-house of a Sabbath day, with her eyes cast down, and after service she glided swiftly down the aisle and was out of the door before the young minister could much more than descend the pulpit stairs, unless he ran an indecorous race.

And young Evelina never at twilight strolled up the road in the direction of Thomas Merriam's home, where she might quite reasonably hope to meet him, since he was wont to go to the store

when the evening stage-coach came in with the
mail from Boston.

Instead she paced the garden paths, or, when
there was not too heavy a dew, rambled across
the fields ; and there was also a lane where she
loved to walk. Whether or not Thomas Merriam
suspected this, or had ever seen, as he passed the
mouth of the lane, the flutter of maidenly draperies in the distance, it so happened that one
evening he also went a-walking there, and met
Evelina. He had entered the lane from the
highway, and she from the fields at the head. So
he saw her first afar off, and could not tell fairly
whether her light muslin skirt might not be only a
white flowering bush. For, since his outlook upon
life had been so full of Evelina, he had found
that often the most common and familiar things
would wear for a second a look of her to startle
him. And many a time his heart had leaped at
the sight of a white bush ahead stirring softly in
the evening wind, and he had thought it might
be she. Now he said to himself impatiently that
this was only another fancy ; but soon he saw
that it was indeed Evelina, in a light muslin
gown, with a little lace kerchief on her head.
His handsome young face was white ; his lips
twitched nervously ; but he reached out and
pulled a spray of white flowers from a bush, and
swung it airily to hide his agitation as he advanced.

As for Evelina, when she first espied Thomas she started and half turned, as if to go back; then she held up her white kerchiefed head with gentle pride and kept on. When she came up to Thomas she walked so far to one side that her muslin skirt was in danger of catching and tearing on the bushes, and she never raised her eyes, and not a flicker of recognition stirred her sweet pale face as she passed him.

But Thomas started as if she had struck him, and dropped his spray of white flowers, and could not help a smothered cry that was half a sob, as he went on, knocking blindly against the bushes. He went a little way, then he stopped and looked back with his piteous hurt eyes. And Evelina had stopped also, and she had the spray of white flowers which he had dropped, in her hand, and her eyes met his. Then she let the flowers fall again, and clapped both her little hands to her face to cover it, and turned to run ; but Thomas was at her side, and he put out his hand and held her softly by her white arm.

"Oh," he panted, "I—did not mean to be— too presuming, and offend you. I—crave your pardon—"

Evelina had recovered herself. She stood with her little hands clasped, and her eyes cast down before him; but not a quiver stirred her pale face, which seemed turned to marble by this last effort of her maiden pride. "I have nothing to pardon," said she. "It was I, whose bold behavior, unbecoming a modest and well-trained young woman, gave rise to what seemed like presumption on your part." The sense of justice was strong within her, but she made her speech haughtily and primly, as if she had learned it by rote from some maiden school-mistress, and pulled her arm away and turned to go; but Thomas's words stopped her.

"Not—unbecoming if it came—from the heart," said he, brokenly, scarcely daring to speak, and yet not daring to be silent.

Then Evelina turned on him, with a sudden strange pride that lay beneath all other pride, and was of a nobler and truer sort. "Do you think I would have given you the look that I did if it had not come from my heart?" she demanded. "What did you take me to be—false and a jilt? I may be a forward young woman, who has over-stepped the bounds of maidenly decorum, and I shall never get over the shame of it, but I am truthful, and I am no jilt." The brilliant color flamed out on Evelina's cheeks. Her blue eyes met Thomas's with that courage of innocence and nature which dares all shame. But it was only for a second; the tears sprung into them. "I beg you to let me go home," she said, pitifully; but Thomas caught her in his arms, and pressed her troubled maiden face against his breast.

"Oh, I love you so!" he whispered—"I love you so, Evelina, and I was afraid you were angry with me for it."

"And I was afraid," she faltered, half weeping and half shrinking from him, "lest you were angry with me for betraying the state of my feelings, when you could not return them." And even then she used that gentle formality of expression with which she had been taught by her maiden preceptors to veil decorously her most ardent emotions. And, in truth, her training stood her in good stead in other ways; for she presently commanded, with that mild dignity of hers which allowed of no remonstrance, that Thomas should take away his arm from her waist, and give her no more kisses for that time.

"It is not becoming for any one," said she, "and much less for a minister of the gospel. And as for myself, I know not what Mistress Perkins would say to me. She has a mind much above me, I fear."

"Mistress Perkins is enjoying her mind in Boston," said Thomas Merriam, with the laugh of a triumphant young lover.

But Evelina did not laugh. "It might be well for both you and me if she were here," said she, seriously. However, she tempered a little her decorous following of Mistress Perkins's precepts, and she and Thomas went hand in hand up the lane and across the fields.

There was no dew that night, and the moon was full. It was after nine o'clock when Thomas left her at the gate in the fence which separated Evelina Adams's garden from the field, and watched her disappear between the flowers. The moon shone full on the garden. Evelina walked as it were over a silver dapple, which her light gown seemed to brush away and dispel for a moment. The bushes stood in sweet mysterious clumps of shadow.

Evelina had almost reached the house, and was close to the great althea bush, which cast a wide circle of shadow, when it seemed suddenly to separate and move into life.

The elder Evelina stepped out from the shadow of the bush. "Is that you, Evelina?" she said, in her soft melancholy voice, which had in it a nervous vibration.

"Yes, Cousin Evelina."

The elder Evelina's pale face, drooped about with gray curls, had an unfamiliar, almost uncanny, look in the moonlight, and might have been the sorrowful visage of some marble nymph, lovelorn, with unceasing grace. "Who — was with you?" she asked.

"The minister," replied young Evelina.

"Did he meet you?"

"He met me in the lane, Cousin Evelina."

"And he walked home with you across the field?"

"Yes, Cousin Evelina."

Then the two entered the house, and nothing more was said about the matter. Young Evelina and Thomas Merriam agreed that their affection was to be kept a secret for a while. "For," said young Evelina, "I cannot leave Cousin Evelina yet a while, and I cannot have her pestered with thinking about it, at least before another spring, when she has the garden fairly growing again."

"That is nearly a whole year; it is August now," said Thomas, half reproachfully, and he tightened his clasp of Evelina's slender fingers.

"I cannot help that," replied Evelina. "It is for you to show Christian patience more than I, Thomas. If you could have seen poor Cousin Evelina, as I have seen her, through the long winter days, when her garden is dead, and she has only the few plants in her window left! When she is not watering and tending them she sits all day in the window and looks out over the garden and the naked bushes and the withered flower-stalks. She used not to be so, but would read her Bible and good books, and busy herself somewhat over fine needle-work, and at one time she was compiling a little floral book, giving a list of the flowers, and poetical selections and sentiments appropriate to each. That was her pastime for three winters, and it is now nearly done;

but she has given that up, and all the rest, and sits there in the window and grows older and feebler until spring. It is only I who can divert her mind, by reading aloud to her and singing; and sometimes I paint the flowers she loves the best on card-board with water-colors. I have a poor skill in it, but Cousin Evelina can tell which flower I have tried to represent, and it pleases her greatly. I have even seen her smile. No, I cannot leave her, nor even pester her with telling her before another spring, and you must wait, Thomas," said young Evelina.

And Thomas agreed, as he was likely to do to all which she proposed which touched not his own sense of right and honor. Young Evelina gave Thomas one more kiss for his earnest pleading, and that night wrote out the tale in her journal. "It may be that I overstepped the bounds of maidenly decorum," wrote Evelina, "but my heart did so entreat me," and no blame whatever did she lay upon Thomas.

Young Evelina opened her heart only to her journal, and her cousin was told nothing, and had little cause for suspicion. Thomas Merriam never came to the house to see his sweetheart; he never walked home with her from meeting. Both were anxious to avoid village gossip, until the elder Evelina could be told.

Often in the summer evenings the lovers met, and strolled hand in hand across the fields, and parted at the garden gate with the one kiss which Evelina allowed, and that was all.

Sometimes when young Evelina came in with her lover's kiss still warm upon her lips the elder Evelina looked at her wistfully, with a strange retrospective expression in her blue eyes, as if she were striving to remember something that the girl's face called to mind. And yet she could have had nothing to remember except dreams.

And once, when young Evelina sat sewing through a long summer afternoon and thinking about her lover, the elder Evelina, who was storing rose leaves mixed with sweet spices in a jar, said, suddenly, " He looks as his father used to."

Young Evelina started. " Whom do you mean, Cousin Evelina?" she asked, wonderingly; for the elder Evelina had not glanced at her, nor even seemed to address her at all.

" Nothing," said the elder Evelina, and a soft flush stole over her withered face and neck, and she sprinkled more cassia on the rose leaves in the jar.

Young Evelina said no more; but she wondered, partly because Thomas was always in her mind, and it seemed to her naturally that nearly everything must have a savor of meaning of him, if her cousin Evelina could possibly have referred to him and his likeness to his father. For it was commonly said that Thomas looked very like his father, although his figure was different. The young man was taller and more firmly built, and he had not the meek forward curve of shoulder which had grown upon his father of late years.

When the frosty nights came Thomas and Evelina could not meet and walk hand in hand over the fields behind the Squire's house, and they very seldom could speak to each other. It was nothing except a "good-day" on the street, and a stolen glance, which set them both a-trembling lest all the congregation had noticed, in the meeting-house. When the winter set fairly in they met no more, for the elder Evelina was taken ill, and her young cousin did not leave her even to go to meeting. People said they guessed it was Evelina Adams's last sickness, and they furthermore guessed that she would divide her property between her cousin Martha Loomis and her two girls and Evelina Leonard, and that Evelina would have the house as her share.

Thomas Merriam heard this last with a satisfaction which he did not try to disguise from himself, because he never dreamed of there being any selfish element in it. It was all for Evelina. Many a time he had looked about the humble house where he had been born, and where he would have to take Evelina after he had married her, and striven to see its poor features with her eyes—not with his, for which familiarity had tempered them. Often, as he sat with his parents in the old sitting-room, in which he had kept so far an unquestioning belief, as in a friend of his childhood, the scales of his own personality would fall suddenly from his eyes. Then he would see, as Evelina, the poor, worn, humble face of his home, and his heart would sink. "I don't see how I ever can bring her here," he thought. He began to save, a few cents at a time out of his pitiful salary, to at least beautify his own chamber a little when Evelina should come. He made up his mind that she should have a little dressing-table, with an oval mirror, and a white muslin frill around it, like one he had seen in Boston. "She shall have that to sit before while she combs her hair," he thought, with defiant tenderness, when he stowed away another shilling in a little box in his trunk. It was money which he ordinarily bestowed upon foreign missions; but his Evelina had come between him and the heathen. To procure some dainty furnishings for her bridal-chamber he took away a good half of his tithes for the spread of the gospel in the dark lands. Now and then his conscience smote him, he felt shamefaced before his deacons, but Evelina kept her first claim. He resolved that another year he would hire a piece of land, and combine farming with his ministerial work, and so try to eke out his salary, and get a little more money to beautify his poor home for his bride.

Now if Evelina Adams had come to the appointed time for the closing of her solitary life, and if her young cousin should inherit a share of her goodly property and the fine old mansion-house, all necessity for anxiety of this kind was over. Young Evelina would not need to be taken away, for the sake of her love, from all these comforts and luxuries. Thomas Merriam rejoiced innocently, without a thought for himself.

In the course of the winter he confided in his father; he couldn't keep it to himself any longer. Then there was another reason. Seeing Evelina so little made him at times almost doubt the reality of it all. There were days when he was depressed, and inclined to ask himself if he had not dreamed it. Telling somebody gave it substance.

His father listened soberly when he told him; he had grown old of late.

"Well," said he, "she 'ain't been used to living the way you have, though you have had advantages that none of your folks ever had; but if she likes you, that's all there is to it, I s'pose."

The old man sighed wearily. He sat in his arm-chair at the kitchen fireplace; his wife had gone in to one of the neighbors, and the two were alone.

"Of course," said Thomas, simply, "if Evelina Adams shouldn't live, the chances are that I shouldn't have to bring her here. She wouldn't have to give up anything on my account—you know that, father."

Then the young man started, for his father turned suddenly on him with a pale, wrathful face. " You ain't countin' on that !" he shouted. "You ain't countin' on that—a son of mine countin' on anything like that !"

Thomas colored. "Why, father," he stammered, " you don't think—you know, it's all for *her*—and they say she can't live anyway. I had never thought of such a thing before. I was wondering how I could make it comfortable for Evelina here."

But his father did not seem to listen. " Countin' on that !" he repeated. " Countin' on a poor old soul, that 'ain't ever had anything to set her heart on but a few posies, dyin' to make room for other folks to have what she's been cheated out on. Countin' on that !" The old man's voice broke into a hoarse sob; he got up, and went hurriedly out of the room.

" Why, father !" his son called after him, in alarm. He got up to follow him, but his father waved him back and shut the door hard.

" Father must be getting childish," Thomas thought, wonderingly. He did not bring up the subject to him again.

Evelina Adams died in March. One morning the bell tolled seventy long melancholy tones before people had eaten their breakfasts. They ran

to their doors and counted. "It's her," they
said, nodding, when they had waited a little after
the seventieth stroke. Directly Mrs. Martha
Loomis and her two girls were seen hustling importantly down the road, with their shawls over
their heads, to the Squire's house. "Mis' Loomis can lay her out," they said. "It ain't likely
that young Evelina knows anything about such
things. Guess she'll be thankful she's got somebody to call on now, if she 'ain't mixed much
with the Loomises." Then they wondered when
the funeral would be, and the women furbished
up their black gowns and bonnets. and even in a
few cases drove to the next town and borrowed
from relatives ; but there was a great disappointment in store for them.

Evelina Adams died on a Saturday. The next
day it was announced from the pulpit that the
funeral would be private, by the particular re-
quest of the deceased. Evelina Adams had carried her delicate seclusion beyond death, to the
very borders of the grave. Nobody, outside the
family, was bidden to the funeral, except the
doctor, the minister, and the two deacons of
the church. They were to be the bearers. The
burial also was to be private, in the Squire's family burial-lot, at the north of the house. The
bearers would carry the coffin across the yard,
and there would not only be no funeral, but no
funeral procession, and no hearse. "It don't

seem scarcely decent," the women whispered to each other ; "and more than all that, she ain't goin' to be *seen*." The deacons' wives were especially disturbed by this last, as they might otherwise have gained many interesting particulars by proxy.

Monday was the day set for the burial. Early in the morning old Thomas Merriam walked feebly up the road to the Squire's house. People noticed him as he passed. "How terrible fast he's grown old lately!" they said. He opened the gate which led into the Squire's front yard with fumbling fingers, and went up the walk to the front door, under the Corinthian pillars, and raised the brass knocker.

Evelina opened the door, and started and blushed when she saw him. She had been crying ; there were red rings around her blue eyes, and her pretty lips were swollen. She tried to smile at Thomas's father, and she held out her hand with shy welcome.

"I want to see her," the old man said, abruptly.

Evelina started, and looked at him wonderingly. "I—don't believe—I know who you mean," said she. "Do you want to see Mrs. Loomis ?"

"No ; I want to see her."

"*Her ?*"

"Yes, *her*."

Evelina turned pale as she stared at him.

There was something strange about his face. "But—Cousin Evelina," she faltered—"she—didn't want— Perhaps you don't know : she left special directions that nobody was to look at her."

" I *want to see her,*" said the old man, and Evelina gave way. She stood aside for him to enter, and led him into the great north parlor, where Evelina Adams lay in her mournful state. The shutters were closed, and one on entering could distinguish nothing but that long black shadow in the middle of the room. Young Evelina opened a shutter a little way, and a slanting shaft of spring sunlight came in and shot athwart the coffin. The old man tiptoed up and leaned over and looked at the dead woman. Evelina Adams had left further instructions about her funeral, which no one understood, but which were faithfully carried out. She wished, she had said, to be attired for her long sleep in a certain rose-colored gown, laid away in rose leaves and lavender in a certain chest in a certain chamber. There were also silken hose and satin shoes with it, and these were to be put on, and a wrought lace tucker fastened with a pearl brooch.

It was the costume she had worn one Sabbath day back in her youth, when she had looked across the meeting-house and her eyes had met young Thomas Merriam's ; but nobody knew nor remembered ; even young Evelina thought it was simply a vagary of her dead cousin's.

"It don't seem to me decent to lay away anybody dressed so," said Mrs. Martha Loomis; "but of course last wishes must be respected."

The two Loomis girls said they were thankful nobody was to see the departed in her rose-colored shroud.

Even old Thomas Merriam, leaning over poor Evelina, cold and dead in the garb of her youth, did not remember it, and saw no meaning in it. He looked at her long. The beautiful color was all faded out of the yellow-white face; the sweet full lips were set and thin; the closed blue eyes sunken in dark hollows; the yellow hair showed a line of gray at the edge of her old woman's cap, and thin gray curls lay against the hollow cheeks. But old Thomas Merriam drew a long breath when he looked at her. It was like a gasp of admiration and wonder; a strange rapture came into his dim eyes; his lips moved as if he whispered to her, but young Evelina could not hear a sound. She watched him, half frightened, but finally he turned to her. "I 'ain't seen her—fairly," said he, hoarsely — "I 'ain't seen her, savin' a glimpse of her at the window, for over forty year, and she 'ain't changed, not a look. I'd have known her anywheres. She's the same as she was when she was a girl. It's wonderful—wonderful!"

Young Evelina shrank a little. "We think she looks natural," she said, hesitatingly.

"She looks jest as she did when she was a girl and used to come into the meetin'-house. She *is* jest the same," the old man repeated, in his eager, hoarse voice. Then he bent over the coffin, and his lips moved again. Young Evelina would have called Mrs. Loomis, for she was frightened, had he not been Thomas's father, and had it not been for her vague feeling that there might be some old story to explain this which she had never heard. "Maybe he was in love with poor Cousin Evelina, as Thomas is with me," thought young Evelina, using her own leaping-pole of love to land straight at the truth. But she never told her surmise to any one except Thomas, and that was long afterwards, when the old man was dead. Now she watched him with her blue dilated eyes. But soon he turned away from the coffin and made his way straight out of the room, without a word. Evelina followed him through the entry and opened the outer door. He turned on the threshold and looked back at her, his face working.

"Don't ye go to lottin' too much on what ye're goin' to get through folks that have died an' not had anything," he said; and he shook his head almost fiercely at her.

"No, I won't. I don't think I understand what you mean, sir," stammered Evelina.

The old man stood looking at her a moment. Suddenly she saw the tears rolling over his old cheeks. "I'm much obliged to ye for lettin' of me see her," he said, hoarsely, and crept feebly down the steps.

Evelina went back trembling to the room where her dead cousin lay, and covered her face, and closed the shutter again. Then she went about her household duties, wondering. She could not understand what it all meant; but one thing she understood—that in some way this old dead woman, Evelina Adams, had gotten immortal youth and beauty in one human heart. "She looked to him just as she did when she was a girl," Evelina kept thinking to herself with awe. She said nothing about it to Mrs. Martha Loomis or her daughters. They had been in the back part of the house, and had not heard old Thomas Merriam come in, and they never knew about it.

Mrs. Loomis and the two girls stayed in the house day and night until after the funeral. They confidently expected to live there in the future. "It isn't likely that Evelina Adams thought a young woman no older than Evelina Leonard could live here alone in this great house with nobody but that old Sarah Judd. It would not be proper nor becoming," said Martha Loomis to her two daughters; and they agreed, and brought over many of their possessions under cover of night to the Squire's house during the interval before the funeral.

But after the funeral and the reading of the

will the Loomises made sundry trips after dusk
back to their old home, with their best petticoats
and cloaks over their arms, and their bonnets
dangling by their strings at their sides. For
Evelina Adams's last will and testament had been
read, and therein provision was made for the con-
tinuance of the annuity heretofore paid them for
their support, with the condition affixed that not
one night should they spend after the reading of
the will in the house known as the Squire Adams
house. The annuity was an ample one, and
would provide the widow Martha Loomis and her
daughters, as it had done before, with all the
needfuls of life; but upon hearing the will they
stiffened their double chins into their kerchiefs
with indignation, for they had looked for more.

Evelina Adams's will was a will of conditions,
for unto it she had affixed two more, and those
affected her beloved cousin Evelina Leonard. It
was notable that "beloved" had not preceded
her cousin Martha Loomis's name in the will. No
pretence of love, when she felt none, had she ever
made in her life. The entire property of Evelina
Adams, spinster, deceased, with the exception of
Widow Martha Loomis's provision, fell to this
beloved young Evelina Leonard, subject to two
conditions—firstly, she was never to enter into
matrimony, with any person whomsoever, at any
time whatsoever; secondly, she was never to let
the said spinster Evelina Adams's garden, situ-

ated at the rear and southward of the house known as the Squire Adams house, die through any neglect of hers. Due allowance was to be made for the dispensations of Providence : for hail and withering frost and long - continued drought, and for times wherein the said Evelina Adams might, by reason of being confined to the house by sickness, be prevented from attending to the needs of the growing plants, and the verdict in such cases was to rest with the minister and the deacons of the church. But should this beloved Evelina love and wed, or should she let, through any wilful neglect, that garden perish in the season of flowers, all that goodly property would she forfeit to a person unknown, whose name, enclosed in a sealed envelope, was to be held meantime in the hands of the executor, who had also drawn up the will, Lawyer Joshua Lang.

There was great excitement in the village over this strange and unwonted will. Some were there who held that Evelina Adams had not been of sound mind, and it should be contested. It was even rumored that Widow Martha Loomis had visited Lawyer Joshua Lang and broached the subject, but he had dismissed the matter peremptorily by telling her that Evelina Adams, spinster, deceased, had been as much in her right mind at the time of drawing the will as anybody of his acquaintance.

" Not setting store by relations, and not want-

ing to have them under your roof, doesn't go far
in law nor common-sense to send folks to the
madhouse," old Lawyer Lang, who was famed
for his sharp tongue, was reported to have said.
However, Mrs. Martha Loomis was somewhat
comforted by her firm belief that either her own
name or that of one of her daughters was in that
sealed envelope kept by Lawyer Joshua Lang
in his strong-box, and by her firm purpose to
watch carefully lest Evelina prove derelict in ful-
filling the two conditions whereby she held the
property.

Larger peep-holes were soon cut away mysteriously in the high arbor-vitæ hedge, and therein
were often set for a few moments, when they
passed that way, the eager eyes of Mrs. Martha or
her daughter Flora or Fidelia Loomis. Frequent
calls they also made upon Evelina, living alone
with the old woman Sarah Judd, who had been
called in during her cousin's illness, and they
strolled into the garden, spying anxiously for
withered leaves or dry stalks. They at every opportunity interviewed the old man who assisted
Evelina in her care of the garden concerning its
welfare. But small progress they made with him,
standing digging at the earth with his spade
while they talked, as if in truth his wits had gone
therein before his body and he would uncover
them.

Moreover, Mrs. Martha Loomis talked much

slyly to mothers of young men, and sometimes with bold insinuations to the young men themselves, of the sad lot of poor young Evelina, condemned to a solitary and loveless life, and of her sweetness and beauty and desirability in herself, although she could not bring the old Squire's money to her husband. And once, but no more than that, she touched lightly upon the subject to the young minister, Thomas Merriam, when he was making a pastoral call.

"My heart bleeds for the poor child living all alone in that great house," said she. And she looked down mournfully, and did not see how white the young minister's face turned. "It seems almost a pity," said she, furthermore— "Evelina is a good housekeeper, and has rare qualities in herself, and so many get poor wives nowadays—that some godly young man should not court her in spite of the will. I doubt, too, if she would not have a happier lot than growing old over that garden, as poor Cousin Evelina did before her, even if she has a fine house to live in and a goodly sum in the bank. She looks pindling enough lately. I'll warrant she has lost a good ten pound since poor Evelina was laid away, and—"

But Thomas Merriam cut her short. "I see no profit in discussing matters which do not concern us," said he, and only his ministerial estate saved him from the charge of impertinence.

As it was, Martha Loomis colored high. "I'll warrant he'll look out which side his bread is buttered on; ministers always do," she said to her daughters after he had gone. She never dreamed how her talk had cut him to the heart.

Had he not seen more plainly than any one else, Sunday after Sunday, when he glanced down at her once or twice cautiously from his pulpit, how weary-looking and thin she was growing? And her bright color was wellnigh gone, and there were pitiful downward lines at the corners of her sweet mouth. Poor young Evelina was fading like one of her own flowers, as if some celestial gardener had failed in his care of her. And Thomas saw it, and in his heart of hearts he knew the reason, and yet he would not yield. Not once had he entered the old Squire's house since he attended the dead Evelina's funeral, and stood praying and eulogizing, with her coffin between him and the living Evelina, with her pale face shrouded in black bombazine. He had never spoken to her since, nor entered the house; but he had written her a letter, in which all the fierce passion and anguish of his heart was cramped and held down by formal words and phrases, and poor young Evelina did not see beneath them. When her lover wrote her that he felt it inconsistent with his Christian duty and the higher aims of his existence to take any further steps towards a matrimonial alliance, she felt merely that Thomas either cared no more for her, or had come to consider, upon due reflection, that she was not fit to undertake the responsible position of a minister's wife. "It may be that in some way I failed in my attendance upon Cousin Evelina," thought poor young Evelina, "or it may be that he thinks I have not enough dignity of character to inspire respect among the older women in the church." And sometimes, with a sharp thrust of misery that shook her out of her enforced patience and meekness, she wondered if indeed her own loving freedom with him had turned him against her, and led him in his later and sober judgment to consider her too light-minded for a minister's wife. "It may be that I was guilty of great indecorum, and almost indeed forfeited my claim to respect for maidenly modesty, inasmuch as I suffered him to give me kisses, and did almost bring myself to return them in kind. But my heart did so entreat me, and in truth it seemed almost like a lack of sincerity for me to wholly withstand it," wrote poor young Evelina in her journal at that time ; and she further wrote : "It is indeed hard for one who has so little knowledge to be fully certain of what is or is not becoming and a Christian duty in matters of this kind ; but if I have in any manner, through my ignorance or unwarrantable affection, failed, and so lost the love and respect of a good man, and the opportunity to become his helpmeet during life, I pray that I may be forgiven—for I sinned not wilfully —that the lesson may be sanctified unto me, and that I may live as the Lord order, in Christian patience and meekness, and not repining." It never occurred to young Evelina that possibly Thomas Merriam's sense of duty might be strengthened by the loss of all her cousin's property should she marry him, and neither did she dream that he might hesitate to take her from affluence into poverty for her own sake. For herself the property, as put in the balance beside her love, was lighter than air itself. It was so light that it had no place in her consciousness. She simply had thought, upon hearing the will, of Martha Loomis and her daughters in possession of the property, and herself with Thomas, with perfect acquiescence and rapture.

Evelina Adams's disapprobation of her marriage, which was supposedly expressed in the will, had indeed, without reference to the property, somewhat troubled her tender heart, but she told herself that Cousin Evelina had not known she had promised to marry Thomas ; that she would not wish her to break her solemn promise. And furthermore, it seemed to her quite reasonable that the condition had been inserted in the will mainly through concern for the beloved garden.

" Cousin Evelina might have thought perhaps I would let the flowers die when I had a husband and children to take care of," said Evelina. And so she had disposed of all the considerations which had disturbed her, and had thought of no others.

She did not answer Thomas's letter. It was so worded that it seemed to require no reply, and she felt that he must be sure of her acquiescence in whatever he thought best. She laid the letter away in a little rosewood box, in which she had always kept her dearest treasures since her school-days. Sometimes she took it out and read it, and it seemed to her that the pain in her heart would put an end to her in spite of all her prayers for Christian fortitude; and yet she could not help reading it again.

It was seldom that she stole a look at her old lover as he stood in the pulpit in the meeting-house, but when she did she thought with an anxious pang that he looked worn and ill, and that night she prayed that the Lord would restore his health to him for the sake of his people.

It was four months after Evelina Adams's death, and her garden was in the full glory of midsummer, when one evening, towards dusk, young Evelina went slowly down the street. She seldom walked abroad now, but kept herself almost as secluded as her cousin had done before her. But that night a great restlessness was upon her, and she put a little black silk shawl over her shoulders and went out. It was quite cool, although it was midsummer. The dusk was deepening fast;

the katydids called back and forth from the wayside bushes. Evelina met nobody for some distance. Then she saw a man coming towards her, and her heart stood still, and she was about to turn back, for she thought for a minute it was the young minister. Then she saw it was his father, and she went on slowly, with her eyes downcast. When she met him she looked up and said good-evening, gravely, and would have passed on, but he stood in her way.

"I've got a word to say to ye, if ye'll listen," he said.

Evelina looked at him tremblingly. There was something strained and solemn in his manner. "I'll hear whatever you have to say, sir," she said.

The old man leaned his pale face over her and raised a shaking forefinger. "I've made up my mind to say something," said he. "I don't know as I've got any right to, and maybe my son will blame me, but I'm goin' to see that you have a chance. It's been borne in upon me that women folks don't always have a fair chance. It's jest this I'm goin' to say: I don't know whether you know how my son feels about it or not. I don't know how open he's been with you. Do you know jest why he quit you?"

Evelina shook her head. "No," she panted —"I don't—I never knew. He said it was his duty."

" Duty can get to be an idol of wood and stone, an' I don't know but Thomas's is," said the old man. " Well, I'll tell you. He don't think it's right for him to marry you, and make you leave that big house, and lose all that money. He don't care anything about it for himself, but it's for you. Did you know that?"

Evelina grasped the old man's arm hard with her little fingers.

" You don't mean that—was why he did it !" she gasped.

" Yes, that was why."

Evelina drew away from him. She was ashamed to have Thomas's father see the joy in her face. "Thank you, sir," she said. " I did not understand. I—will write to him."

" Maybe my son will think I have done wrong coming betwixt him and his idees of duty," said old Thomas Merriam, " but sometimes there's a good deal lost for lack of a word, and I wanted you to have a fair chance an' a fair say. It's been borne in upon me that women folks don't always have it. Now you can do jest as you think best, but you must remember one thing—riches ain't all. A little likin' for you that's goin' to last, and keep honest and faithful to you as long as you live, is worth more ; an' it's worth more to women folks than 'tis to men, an' it's worth enough to them. My son's poorly. His mother and I are worried about him. He don't eat nor sleep—walks his chamber nights. His mother don't know what the matter is, but he let on to me some time since."

"I'll write a letter to him," gasped Evelina again. "Good-night, sir." She pulled her little black silk shawl over her head and hastened home, and all night long her candle burned, while her weary little fingers toiled over pages of foolscap-paper to convince Thomas Merriam fully, and yet in terms not exceeding maidenly reserve, that the love of his heart and the companionship of his life were worth more to her than all the silver and gold in the world. Then the next morning she despatched it, all neatly folded and sealed, and waited.

It was strange that a letter like that could not have moved Thomas Merriam, when his heart too pleaded with him so hard to be moved. But that might have been the very reason why he could withstand her, and why the consciousness of his own weakness gave him strength. Thomas Merriam was one, when he had once fairly laid hold of duty, to grasp it hard, although it might be to his own pain and death, and maybe to that of others. He wrote to poor young Evelina another letter, in which he emphasized and repeated his strict adherence to what he believed the line of duty in their separation, and ended it with a prayer for her welfare and happiness, in which, indeed, for a second, the passionate heart of the

man showed forth. Then he locked himself in
his chamber, and nobody ever knew what he suffered there. But one pang he did not suffer
which Evelina would have suffered in his place.
He mourned not over nor realized the grief of her
tender heart when she should read his letter,
otherwise he could not have sent it. He writhed
under his own pain alone, and his duty hugged
him hard, like the iron maiden of the old tort-
ures, but he would not yield.

As for Evelina, when she got his letter, and
had read it through, she sat still and white for a
long time, and did not seem to hear when old
Sarah Judd spoke to her. But at last she rose
and went to her chamber, and knelt down, and
prayed for a long time; and then she went out
in the garden and cut all the most beautiful flowers, and tied them in wreaths and bouquets, and
carried them out to the north side of the house,
where her cousin Evelina was buried, and covered her grave with them. And then she knelt
down there and hid her face among them, and
said, in a low voice, as if in a listening ear, "I
pray you, Cousin Evelina, forgive me for what I
am about to do."

And then she returned to the house, and sat at
her needle-work as usual; but the old woman
kept looking at her, and asking if she were sick,
for there was a strange look in her face.

She and old Sarah Judd had always their tea

at five o'clock, and put the candles out at nine, and this night they did as they were wont. But at one o'clock in the morning young Evelina stole softly down the stairs with her lighted candle, and passed through into the kitchen; and a half-hour after she came forth into the garden, which lay in full moonlight, and she had in her hand a steaming teakettle, and she passed around among the shrubs and watered them, and a white cloud of steam rose around them. Back and forth she went to the kitchen; for she had heated the great copper wash-kettle full of water; and she watered all the shrubs in the garden, moving amid curling white wreaths of steam, until the water was gone. And then she set to work and tore up by the roots with her little hands and trampled with her little feet all the beautiful tender flower-beds; all the time weeping, and moaning softly: "Poor Cousin Evelina! poor Cousin Evelina! Oh, forgive me, poor Cousin Evelina!"

And at dawn the garden lay in ruin, for all the tender plants she had torn up by the roots and trampled down, and all the stronger-rooted shrubs she had striven to kill with boiling water and salt.

Then Evelina went into the house, and made herself tidy as well as she could when she trembled so, and put her little shawl over her head, and went down the road to the Merriams' house. It was so early the village was scarcely astir, but

there was smoke coming out of the kitchen chimney at the Merriams'; and when she knocked,
Mrs. Merriam opened the door at once, and stared
at her.

"Is Sarah Judd dead?" she cried; for her first
thought was that something must have happened
when she saw the girl standing there with her
wild pale face.

"I want to see the minister," said Evelina,
faintly, and she looked at Thomas's mother with
piteous eyes.

"Be you sick?" asked Mrs. Merriam. She laid
a hard hand on the girl's arm, and led her into
the sitting-room, and put her into the rocking-
chair with the feather cushion. "You look real
poorly," said she. "Sha'n't I get you a little of
my elderberry wine?"

"I want to see him," said Evelina, and she almost sobbed.

"I'll go right and speak to him," said Mrs.
Merriam. "He's up, I guess. He gets up early
to write. But hadn't I better get you something
to take first? You do look sick."

But Evelina only shook her head. She had her
face covered with her hands, and was weeping
softly. Mrs. Merriam left the room, with a long
backward glance at her. Presently the door opened and Thomas came in. Evelina stood up before
him. Her pale face was all wet with tears, but
there was an air of strange triumph about her.

"THE LORD MAKE ME WORTHY
OF THEE, EVELINA"

"The garden is dead," said she.

"What do you mean?" he cried out, staring at her, for indeed he thought for a minute that her wits had left her.

"The garden is dead," said she. "Last night I watered the roses with boiling water and salt, and I pulled the other flowers up by their roots. The garden is dead, and I have lost all Cousin Evelina's money, and it need not come between us any longer." She said that, and looked up in his face with her blue eyes, through which the love of the whole race of loving women from which she had sprung, as well as her own, seemed to look, and held out her little hands; but even then Thomas Merriam could not understand, and stood looking at her.

"Why—did you do it?" he stammered.

"Because you would have me no other way, and — I couldn't bear that anything like that should come between us," she said, and her voice shook like a harp-string, and her pale face went red, then pale again.

But Thomas still stood staring at her. Then her heart failed her. She thought that he did not care, and she had been mistaken. She felt as if it were the hour of her death, and turned to go. And then he caught her in his arms.

"Oh," he cried, with a great sob, "the Lord make me worthy of thee, Evelina!"

There had never been so much excitement in

the village as when the fact of the ruined garden came to light. Flora Loomis, peeping through the hedge on her way to the store, had spied it first. Then she had run home for her mother, who had in turn sought Lawyer Lang, panting bonnetless down the road. But before the lawyer had started for the scene of disaster, the minister, Thomas Merriam, had appeared, and asked for a word in private with him. Nobody ever knew just what that word was, but the lawyer was singularly uncommunicative and reticent as to the ruined garden.

"Do you think the young woman is out of her mind?" one of the deacons asked him, in a whisper.

"I wish all the young women were as much in their minds; we'd have a better world," said the lawyer, gruffly.

"When do you think we can begin to move in here?" asked Mrs. Martha Loomis, her wide skirts sweeping a bed of uprooted verbenas.

"When your claim is established," returned the lawyer, shortly, and turned on his heel and went away, his dry old face scanning the ground like a dog on a scent. That afternoon he opened the sealed document in the presence of witnesses, and the name of the heir to whom the property fell was disclosed. It was "Thomas Merriam, the beloved and esteemed minister of this parish." and young Evelina would gain her wealth instead of losing it by her marriage. And furthermore, after the declaration of the name of the heir was this added : "This do I in the hope and belief that neither the greed of riches nor the fear of them shall prevent that which is good and wise in the sight of the Lord, and with the surety that a love which shall triumph over so much in its way shall endure, and shall be a blessing and not a curse to my beloved cousin, Evelina Leonard."

Thomas Merriam and Evelina were married before the leaves fell in that same year, by the minister of the next village, who rode over in his chaise, and brought his wife, who was also a bride, and wore her wedding-dress of a pink and pearl shot silk. But young Evelina wore the blue bridal array which had been worn by old Squire Adams's bride, all remodelled daintily to suit the fashion of the times; and as she moved, the fragrances of roses and lavender of the old summers during which it had been laid away were evident, like sweet memories.

A NEW ENGLAND PROPHET

At half-past six o'clock a little company of people passed down the village street in the direction of the Lennox farm-house.

They advanced in silence, stepping along the frozen ridges of the road. It was cold, but there was no snow. There was a young moon shining through thin white clouds like nebulæ.

Now and then, as the company went on, new recruits were gathered from the scattered houses. A man would emerge darkly from a creaking gate, with maybe a second and third dark figure following, with a flirt of feminine draperies. "There's Deacon Scranton," or "There's Thomas Jennings and his wife and Ellen," the people would murmur to one another.

Once a gleam of candle-light from an open door lay across the road in advance, and wavered into darkness with a slam of the door when the company drew near. Then a solitary woman came ponderously down the front walk, seeming to jar the frozen earth with the jolt of her great femi-

184

nine bulk. " There's Abby Mosely," somebody
muttered. Sometimes two young girls fluttered
out of a door-yard, clinging together with nervous
giggles and outcries, which were soon hushed.
They moved along with the others, their little
cold fingers clinging together with a rigid clutch.
It was as if a strange, solemn atmosphere sur-
rounded this group moving along the country
road in the starlit night. Whoever came into
their midst felt it, and his emotions changed involuntarily as respiration changes on a mountain-
top.

When the party reached a windy hill-top in
sight of the lighted windows of the Lennox house
in the valley below, it numbered nearly twenty.
Half-way down the hill somebody else joined
them. He had been standing ahead of them,
waiting in the long shadow of a poplar, and they
had not discerned him until they were close to
him. Then he stepped forward and the shadow
of the tree was left motionless. The young girls
half screamed, he appeared so suddenly, and their
nerves were strained. The elders made a solemn
hushed murmur of greeting. They knew as soon
as he moved that he was Isaac Penfield. He had
a martial carriage of his shoulders, he was a captain in the militia, and he wore an ash-colored
cloak, which distinguished him.

The young girls cast glances, bolder from the
darkness, towards his stately ash-colored shoul-

ders and the pale gleam of his face. Not one of them who had not her own lover but had her innocent secret dreams about this Isaac Penfield. Now, had a light shone out suddenly in the darkness, their dreams would have shown in their faces.

One slender girl slunk softly around in the rear darkness and crept so close to Isaac Penfield that his ash-colored cloak, swinging out in the wind, brushed her cheek. He did not notice her; indeed, after his first murmur of salutation, he did not speak to any one.

They all went in silence down the hill, and flocked into the yard of the Lennox house. There was a red flicker of light in the kitchen windows from the great hearth fire, but a circle of dark heads and shoulders hid the fire itself from the new-comers. There was evidently a number of people inside.

Deacon Scranton raised the knocker, and the door was opened immediately. Melissa Lennox stood there holding a candle in a brass candlestick, with the soft light streaming up on her fair face. She looked through it with innocent, anxious blue eyes at the company. "Won't you walk in?" she said, tremulously, and the people passed into the south entry, and through the door on the left into the great Lennox kitchen. Some dozen persons who had come from the other end of the village were already there.

Isaac Penfield entered last. Melissa did not see him until he stepped suddenly within her radius of candle-light. Then she started, and bent her head before him, blushing. The candle shook in her outstretched hand.

Isaac Penfield took the candle without a word and set it on the stairs. Then he took Melissa's slim right hand in his, and stood a moment looking down at her bent head, with its parted gloss of hair. His forehead was frowning, and yet he half smiled with tender triumph.

"Come out in the front yard with me a moment," he whispered. He pulled her with gentle force towards the door, and the girl yielded, after a faint murmur of expostulation.

Out in the front yard Isaac Penfield folded a corner of his ash-colored cloak around Melissa's slender shoulders.

"Now I want you to tell me, Melissa," he whispered. "You are not still carried away by all this?" He jerked his head towards the kitchen windows.

Melissa trembled against the young man's side under the folds of his cloak.

"You are not, after all I said to you, Melissa?"

She nodded against his breast, with a faint sob.

"I hoped you would do as I asked you, and cut loose from this folly," Isaac Penfield said, sternly.

"Father—says—it's true. Oh, I am afraid—I am afraid! My sins are so great, and I cannot hide from the eyes of the Lord. I am afraid!"

Isaac Penfield tightened his clasp of the girl's trembling figure, and bent his head low down over hers. "Melissa, dear, can't you listen to me?" he whispered.

Suddenly the kitchen door opened, and a new light streamed across the entry.

"Melissa, where be you?" called a woman's voice, high-pitched and melancholy.

"There's mother calling," Melissa said, in a frightened whisper, and she broke away and ran into the house.

Her mother stood in the kitchen door. "Where have you been?" she began. Then she stopped, and looked at Isaac Penfield with a half-shrinking, half-antagonistic air. This stalwart young man, radiant with the knowledge of his own strength, represented to this delicate woman, who was held to the earth more by the tension of nerves than the weight of matter, the very pride of life, the material power which she was to fear and fight for herself and for her daughter.

"I thought I would step into your meeting to-night, if I were permitted," Isaac Penfield said.

Mrs. Lennox looked at him with deep blue eyes under high, thin temples. "All are permitted who listen to the truth with the right spirit," said she, and turned shortly and glided into the kitchen. Melissa and Isaac followed.

The company sat in wide semicircles, three deep, before the fire. In the open space between the first semicircle and the fire, his wide arm-chair on the bricks of the broad hearth, half facing the company, sat Solomon Lennox. Near him sat his deaf-and-dumb son Alonzo. He held up a large slate so the firelight fell upon it, and marked upon it with a grating pencil. He screwed his face with every stroke, so it seemed that one watching attentively might discern the picture itself from his changing features.

Alonzo Lennox was fourteen years old, but he looked no more than ten, and he had been deaf and dumb from his birth. The firelight gave a reddish tinge to his silvery blond hair, spreading out stiffly from the top of his head over his ears like the thatch of a hut. His delicate irregular profile bent over the slate; now and then a spasm of silent merriment shook his narrow chest, and the surrounding people looked at him with awe. They regarded it as the mystic ecstasy of a seer.

Melissa and her mother had slid softly through the semicircles to the chairs they had left. Isaac Penfield stood on the outskirts, towering over all the people, refusing a seat which somebody offered him. He threw off his ash-colored cloak and held it on his arm. His costume of fine broadcloth and flowered satin and glittering but-

tons surpassed any there, as did his face and his
height and his carriage; and, more than all, he
stood among the others raised upon a spiritual
eminence, unseen, but none the less real, which
his ancestors had reared for him before his birth.
The Penfield name had been a great one in that
vicinity for three generations. Once Penfields
had owned the larger part of the township.
Isaac's father, and his grandfather before him,
had been esquires, and held as nearly the position of lords of this little village as was possible
in New England. Now this young man was the
last of his race, living, with his housekeeper and
an old servant, in the Penfield homestead; and
the village adulation which had been accorded
to his ancestors was his also in a large measure.

To-night, as he entered, people glanced at him,
away from Alonzo and his slate, but only for a
moment. The matter under discussion that night
was too solemn and terrible to be lost sight of
long.

In about ten minutes after Isaac Penfield entered, the boy gave a shout, grating and hideous,
with a discord of human thoughts and senses in
it. A shudder passed over the company like a
wind.

Alonzo Lennox sprang up and waved the slate,
and his father reached out for it. "Give it to
me," he demanded, sternly, as if the boy could
hear. But Alonzo gave another shout, and leaped

aside, and waved the slate out of his father's reach. Then he danced lightly up and down on the tips of his toes, shaking his head and flinging out fantastic heels. His shock of hair flew out wildly, and looked like a luminous crown ; the firelight struck his dilated eyes, and they gleamed red.

The people watched him with sobbing breaths and pale faces, all except Isaac Penfield and one other. Isaac stood looking at him, with his mouth curling in a scornful smile. Solomon Lennox stood aside with a startled air, then he caught the boy firmly by the arm and grasped the slate.

Alonzo grinned impishly in his father's face, then he let go the slate, and sank down on his stool in the chimney-corner. There he sat submissive and inactive, except for the cunning, sharp flash of his blue eyes under his thatch of hair.

Solomon Lennox held the slate to the light and looked at it, while the people waited breathless, their pale intent faces bent forward. Then he handed the slate, without a word, to the man at the end of the first semicircle, and it was circulated through the entire company. As one passed the slate to another a shuddering thrill like an electric shock seemed to be passed with it, and there was a faint murmur of horror.

Isaac Penfield held the slate longest, and examined it closely. Drawn with a free hand, which certainly gave evidence of some inborn artistic skill aside from aught else, were great sweeping curves of wings upbearing an angel with a trumpet at his mouth. Under his feet were lashing tongues as of flames, with upturned faces of agony in the midst of them. And everywhere, between the wings and the angel and the flames and the faces, were, in groups of five, those grotesque little symbols of the sun, a disk with human features therein, which one sees in the almanacs.

After Isaac Penfield had finished looking at the mystic slate he passed it to Solomon Lennox's elder brother, Simeon, who sat at his right. The old man's hard shaven jaws widened in a sardonic grin; his small black eyes twinkled derisively over the drawings. "Pretty pictures," he said, half aloud. Then he passed the slate along with a contemptuous chuckle, which was heard in the solemn stillness all over the room.

Solomon Lennox gave a furious glance in his brother's direction. "This is no time nor season for scoffers!" cried he. And his voice seemed to shock the air like a musket-shot.

Simeon Lennox chuckled again. Solomon's right hand clinched. He arose; then sat down again, with his mouth compressed. He sat still until the slate had gone its rounds and returned to the boy, who sat contemplating it with un-

couth delight; then he stood up, and the words
flowed from his mouth in torrents. Never at a
loss for subject-matter of speech was Solomon
Lennox. By the fluency of his discourse he
might well have been thought inspired. He
spoke of visions of wings and holy candlesticks
and beasts and cups of abomination as if he had
with his own eyes seen them like the prophet of
old. He expounded strange and subtle mathe-
matical calculations and erratic interpretations
of history as applied to revelation with a fervor
which brought conviction to his audience. He
caught the slate from his deaf-and-dumb son, and
explained the weird characters thereon. The
five suns were five days. Five times the sun
should arise in the east, as it had done from the
creation; then should the angel, upborne on
those great white wings, sound his trumpet, and
the flames burst forth from the lower pit, and
those upturned faces in the midst of them gnash
with despair.

"Repent, for the day of the Lord is at hand!"
shouted Solomon Lennox at the close of his ar-
guments, and his voice itself rang like a trumpet
full of all intonations and reverberations, of awe
and dread. "Repent, for the great and dreadful
day of the Lord is at hand! Repent while there
is yet time, while there is yet a foothold on the
shore of the lake of fire! Repent, repent! Prepare
your ascension robes! Renounce the world, and

all the lust and the vanity thereof! Repent, for the day of judgment is here! Soon shall ye choke with the smoke of the everlasting burning, soon shall your eyes be scorched with the fiery scroll of the heavens, your ears be deafened with the blast of the trumpet of wrath, and the cry against you of your own sins! Repent, repent, repent!"

Solomon Lennox's slight figure writhed with his own emotion as with internal fire; the veins swelled out on his high bald forehead; his eyes blazed with fanatical light. Aside from the startling nature of his discourse, he himself was a marvel, and a terror to his neighbors. His complete deviation from a former line of life produced among them the horror of the supernatural. He affected them like his own ghost. He had always been a man of few and quiet words, who had never expressed his own emotions in public beyond an inaudible, muttered prayer at a conference meeting, and now this flood of fiery eloquence from him seemed like a very convulsion of human nature.

When a great physical malady is epidemic there are often isolated cases in remote localities whose connection with the main disturbance cannot be established. So in this little New England village, far from a railroad, scarcely reached by the news of the day, Solomon Lennox had developed within himself, with seeming spontaneity, some of the startling tenets of Joseph Miller, and had established his own small circle of devoted disciples and followers. It was as if some germs of a great spiritual disturbance had sought, through some unknown medium, this man's mind as their best ripening place.

After Solomon had arisen one night in conference meeting and poured forth his soul to his startled neighbors in a strain of fiery prophecy, Millerite publications had been sent for, and he had strengthened his own theories with those of the original leader, although in many respects his maintained a distinct variance.

The effect of Solomon's prophecies had been greatly enhanced by the drawings of his deaf-and-dumb son. Alonzo Lennox's slate, covered with rude representations of beasts and trumpets and winged creatures—the weird symbolic figures of the prophet Daniel — had aroused a tumult of awe and terror in the village. And the more so because the boy had never learned the language of the deaf and dumb, and had no ordinary and comprehensible means of acquiring information upon such topics.

To-night, as his father spoke, he kept his blue eyes upon his face with such a keen look that it seemed almost impossible that he did not hear and comprehend every word. Unbelievers in this new movement were divided between the opinion that Lonny Lennox had heard more than folks had given him credit for right along, and the one that he understood by some strange power which the loss of his other faculties had sharpened.

"The boy has developed the sixth sense," Isaac Penfield thought as he watched his intent face upturned towards his father's; and he also thought impatiently that he should be cuffed and sent to bed for his uncanny sharpness. He grew more and more indignant as the time went on and the excitement deepened. He watched Melissa grow paler and paler, and finally press her slender hands over her face, and shake with sobs, and made a sudden motion as if he would go to her. Then he restrained himself, and muttered something between his teeth.

Old Simeon Lennox watched him curiously, then he hit him in the side with a sharp elbow. "Made up your mind to go up in our family chariot on the last day?" he whispered, with a hoarse whistle of breath in Isaac's ear. Then he leaned back, with a long cackle of laughter in his throat, which was unheard in the din of his brother's raging voice and the responsive groans and sobs.

Isaac Penfield colored, and kept his eyes straight forward and his head up with a haughty air. Presently the old man nudged him again, with the sharpness of malice protected by helplessness. "Guess," he whispered, craning up to the young man's handsome, impatient face—

"guess you 'ain't much opinion of all this darned tomfoolery neither."

Isaac shook his head fiercely.

" Well," said the old man, " let 'em go it," and he cackled with laughter again.

After Solomon Lennox had finished his fervid appeal, two or three offered prayers, and many testified and confessed sins, and professed repentance, and terror of the wrath to come, in hoarse, strained voices, half drowned by sobs and cries.

It was nearly midnight before Solomon Lennox declared the meeting at a close, and recommended the brethren and sisters to repair to their homes, not to sleep, but to pray, and appointed another session for the next forenoon, for these meetings of terror-stricken and contrite souls were held three times a day—morning, afternoon, and evening. In those days the housewives' kitchen tables were piled high with unwashed dishes, the hearths were unswept and the fires low, the pantry shelves were bare, and often the children went to bed with only the terrors of the judgment for sustenance.

In those days the cattle grew lean, and stood lowing piteously long after nightfall at the pasture bars. Even the horses turned in their stalls at every footfall and whinnied for food. Men lost all thought for their earthly goods in their fierce concern for their own souls.

The people flocked out of Solomon Lennox's

kitchen, some with rapt eyes, some white-faced and trembling, huddling together as if with a forlorn hope that human companionship might avail somewhat even against divine judgment. The deaf-and-dumb boy went sleepily out of the room and up-stairs with his candle, leaving his slate on the hearthstone. Isaac Penfield stood a few minutes looking irresolutely at Melissa, who sat still with her hands pressed tightly over her face, as if she were weeping. Her mother stood near her, talking to Abby Mosely, who was Simeon Lennox's housekeeper. The woman was fairly gasping with emotion; her broad shawled bosom heaved.

"Repent!" cried Mrs. Lennox, loud, in her ears, like an echo of her husband. "Repent; there is yet time! There are five days before the heavens open! Repent!" Her nervous hands served to intensify her weak, straining voice. They pointed and threatened in the woman's piteous, scared face. Isaac started to approach Melissa; then her mother half turned and seemed to shriek out her warning cry towards him, and he tossed his gray cloak over his shoulders, strode out of the room, and out of the house.

Old Simeon Lennox lingered behind the others.

"I'm a-comin' right along, Abby," he called to his housekeeper when she started to leave the room. "If ye go to bed afore I come, mind ye

198

put the cat out, so she won't get afoul of that pig meat in the pantry." Simeon spoke with cool disregard of the distressed sobs and moans with which the woman was making her exit.

"D'ye hear what I say, Abby?" he called, sharply, when she did not reply.

The housekeeper groaned a faint assent over her shoulder as she crossed the threshold.

"Well, mind ye don't forgit it," said Simeon, "for I tell ye what 'tis, if that cat does git afoul of that pig meat, there'll be a jedgement afore Thursday."

The old man clamped leisurely across the room, drew an arm-chair close to the fire, and settled into it with a grunting yawn.

"Fire feels good," he remarked. His voice was thick, for he had tobacco in his mouth.

"Woe be unto you, Simeon Lennox, if you can still think of the comfort of your poor body which will soon be ashes," cried his sister-in-law. She waved before him like a pale flame; her white face seemed fairly luminous.

Simeon shifted his tobacco into one cheek as he stared at her. "You'd better go to bed, Sophy Anne; you're gittin' highstericky," said he, and chewed again.

"Woe be unto you, fer the bed you shall lie on, unless you repent, Simeon Lennox!"

"Look at here, Sophy Anne," said Simeon, "ain't you got no mince-pies in the house?"

Mrs. Lennox looked at him, speechless, for a moment.

"If you have," Simeon went on, "I wish you'd give me a piece. I 'ain't had no mince-pie fit to eat I dun'no' when. Abby Mosely wa'n't never much of a cook, and sence she's took to goin' to your meetin' here three times a day, it's much as ever's I get anything. It ain't no more'n fair, Sophy Anne, that you should give me a piece of mince-pie, if you've got any."

Mrs. Lennox broke in upon him with a cry which was almost a shriek. "I shall make no more pies in this world, Simeon Lennox. Woe be unto you! Woe be unto you if you think of such things in the face of death and eternal condemnation!"

Solomon Lennox had followed the departing people into the yard. His exhorting voice could still be heard out there, for the doors were open.

Simeon looked around and shivered. "If you 'ain't got no mince-pie, I wish you'd shet that door, Sophy Anne," he said.

Sophia Anne Lennox stood looking at him for a minute. He chuckled in her face. She snatched a candle from the shelf and went out of the room with an air of desperation.

Melissa rose up and crept after her, her face like a drooping white flower, gliding so closely in her mother's wake that she seemed to have no individual motion of her own. Simeon looked hard at her as she went.

"Sophy Anne is wiry," he said, when his brother came in. "She'll go it all right if the wires don't snap, an' I reckon they won't; but you'd better look out for Melissy. She can't stan' such tearin' work as this very long. She'll have a fever or somethin'."

"What matters that?" cried Solomon. "What matters any tribulation of the flesh when the end of all flesh is at hand?" His voice was hoarse with his long clamor. He leaned over and shook a nervous fist impressively before his brother's face.

Simeon chewed on, and looked at the fist without winking. "You don't mean to say, Solomon Lennox," said he at length, "that you believe all this darned tomfoolery?"

His brother looked at him with solemn wrath. "Do I believe revelation and the prophets?" he cried. "Woe be unto all scoffers, even though they be my own flesh and blood!"

"Now, Solomon, I'll jest stump ye to point out any passage in the Scripturs that says, up an' down, square an' fair, that the world's comin' to an end next Thursday. I'll jest stump ye to do it."

"'There are passages that point to the truth, and I have repeated them to-night," replied Solomon, hotly.

"Passages that ye've had to twist hind-side

foremost, an' bottom-side up, an' add, an' sub-
tract, an' divide, an' multiply, an' hammer, an'
saw, an' bile down, an' take to a grist-mill, afore
you got at the meanin' you wanted," returned his
brother, contemptuously. " That ain't the kind
of passage I'm after. There's too much two-
facedness an' double-dealin' about the Scripturs
anyway, judgin' by some of you folks. What I
want is a square up an' down passage that says,
without no chance of its meanin' anything else,
'The world is comin' to an end next week Thursday.' I stump ye to show me such a passage as
that. *Ye can't do it!*"

The habits of a lifetime are strong even in
strained and exalted states, acting like the lash
of a familiar whip. Solomon Lennox was the
younger brother; all his life he had borne a certain docility of attitude towards Simeon, which
asserted itself now.

The fervid orator stood for a moment silent
before this sceptical, sneering elder brother. "I'd
like to know how you account for Lonny's drawin's," he said at length, in a tone which he might
have used when bullied by Simeon in their boy-
hood.

"Drawin's," drawled Simeon, and sarcasm itself seemed to hiss in the final s—" dr-r-awin's !
The little scamp is sharp as steel, an' he's watched
an' he's eyed till he's put two an' two together.
It's easy enough to account for the drawin's. The

air here has been so thick lately with wings an' wheels an' horns an' trumpets an' everlastin' fire that anybody that wa'n't an idgit could breathe it in. An' I miss my guess if his mother 'ain't showed him the picturs in the big Bible mor'n once when you've been talkin', an' pointed out the hearth fire an' the candlesticks an' the powder-horn. Sophy Anne's sharp, an' she's done more to learn that boy than anybody knows of, though I've got my doubts now as to how straight he's really got it in his mind. Lord, them drawin's ain't nothin'. Solomon Lennox, you can't look me in the face an' say that you actilly believe all this darned tomfoolery!"

Solomon for these few minutes had been on the old level of a brotherly argument, but now he arose suddenly to his latter heights.

"I believe that the end of the world is near, that the great and dreadful day of the Lord is at hand, accordin' to prophecy and revelation," he proclaimed, and his eyes shone under his high forehead as under a majestic dome of thought and inspiration.

Simeon whistled. "Ye don't, though. Look at here, Solomon; tell ye what I'll do. I'll put ye to the test. Look at here, you say the world's comin' to an end next Thursday. Well, it stands to reason if it is, that you 'ain't got no more need of temporal goods. S'pose—you give me a deed of this 'ere farm?"

Solomon stared at his brother.

Simeon shook his fist at him slowly. "*Ye won't do it*," he said, with a triumphant chuckle.

" I *will* do it."

" Git Lawyer Bascombe to draw up the papers to-morrow ?"

" *I will.*"

" Me to take possession by daylight next Friday mornin', if the world don't come to an end Thursday night ?"

" *Yes*," replied Solomon, hurling the word at his brother like a stone.

Simeon got up and buttoned his coat over his lean chest. " Well," said he, " I've had pretty hard luck. I've lost three wives, and I've been burnt out twice, an' the last house ain't none too tight. I'll move right in here next Friday mornin' at daylight. Mebbe I'll get married again."

" Much good will the heaping up of barns an' storehouses do when you hear the voice of the Lord saying, ' Thou fool, this night shall thy soul be required of thee,' " returned his brother ; but he spoke the fervid words with a certain feebleness. All his life since he was a boy had Solomon Lennox toiled and saved to own this noble farm. The bare imagination of giving it up to another cost him much, although he firmly believed that in a week's space it would be only a modicum of the blackened ashes of a world. He

204

stood the test of his faith, but he felt the scorch of sacrificial flame.

"It ain't me that's the fool," said Simeon, shrugging himself into his great-coat. "I ain't goin' to hang back with my soul when it's required of me, but I ain't goin' to keep chuckin' of it in the face of the Lord afore He's ready for it, like some folks I know. Them's the fools. When 'll you be down to Lawyer Bascombe's to-morrow, Solomon, to deed away these barns an' storehouses that you 'ain't no more use for ?"

"I'll be down there at nine o'clock to-morrow mornin'."

"All right; you can count on me," said Simeon. He went out, and Solomon bolted the door after him promptly. But he had no sooner returned to the kitchen than there came a sharp tap on the window, and there was Simeon's hard leering old face pressed against the pane. "You'll —have—to—fetch Sophy Anne down there to-morrow," he called. "She'll—have to sign that deed too, or it won't stan'."

"All right," shouted Solomon, and the face at the window, with a parting nod, disappeared.

Lawyer Bascombe's office was in the centre of the village, over the store. A steep flight of stairs at the right of the store led to it. Up these stairs, at nine o'clock the next morning, climbed Solomon Lennox and his wife Sophia Anne, with pale devoted faces, and signed away

205

all their earthly goods as an evidence of their faith.

In some way the matter had become known in the village. When Solomon and Sophia Anne came down the stairs there was quite a crowd before the door, standing back with awed curiosity to let them pass. Simeon Lennox did not leave at once after the signing of the deed. When he appeared in the doorway with a roll of paper in his hand the crowd had dispersed.

Without any doubt this act of Solomon Lennox and his wife materially strengthened their cause. When it became known that they had actually signed away their property in their confidence that days of property-holding were over, even scoffers began to look serious. That evening the meeting at Solomon Lennox's house numbered a third more than usual. The next evening it was doubled, and the best room as well as the kitchen was filled. Solomon stood at the foot of the stairs in the entry between the rooms and exhorted, while the deaf-and-dumb boy's slate circulated among the awe-stricken people.

Isaac Penfield came to no more meetings, and he did not see Melissa again until Tuesday. Late Tuesday afternoon she went up to the village store with a basket of eggs. The days of barter were nearly over, as she had been taught to believe, but there was no molasses in the house, and the poor deaf-and-dumb boy was weeping for it with uncouth grief, and could not be comforted by the prospect of eternal joys. When Melissa came out of the store with the bottle of molasses in her basket, Isaac Penfield's bay mare and chaise were drawn up before the platform, and Isaac stood waiting. Melissa started and colored when she saw him.

"Get in, please," he said, motioning her towards the chaise.

She looked at him falteringly.

"Get in, please, Melissa; I want to speak to you."

The bay mare was restive, tossing her head and pawing with one delicate fore foot. Isaac could scarcely keep her quiet until Melissa got in. When he took the reins she gave a leap forward, and the chaise swung about with a lurch. Isaac threw himself back and held the reins taut; the mare flew down the road, pulling hard on her bits; the chaise rocked high on the frozen road. Melissa sat still, her delicate face retired within the dark depths of her silk hood.

Isaac did not speak to her until they reached the foot of a long hill. "I want to ask you something," he said then, with a wary eye still on the straining shoulders of the mare. "I want to ask you again to give this up."

Melissa did not speak.

"Won't you promise me?"

"I can't," she said, faintly.

"You can if you will." Suddenly Isaac leaned over her. "Won't you promise *me*, Melissa?"

She shrank away from him. "I—can't. I believe father."

"Melissa, you don't."

"I do," said she, with a despairing sob.

Isaac Penfield bent his face down close to hers. "Can't you believe me as well as your father? Melissa, look at me."

Melissa bent her head down over her hands.

"Look at me, Melissa."

She raised her head slowly as if there were a constraining hand under her chin, and her eyes met his.

"Can't you, Melissa?"

Fair locks of hair fell over the girl's gentle cheeks; her soft mouth quivered. It seemed as if her piteous blue eyes were only upheld by the look in the young man's, and as if all the individual thought and purpose in her face and her whole soul were being overcast by his imperious will, but she shook her head.

"Can't you, Melissa?"

She shook her head again.

Isaac Penfield's face turned white. He touched the whip to the mare, and she gave a sharp bound forward. They had not much farther to go. Neither of them spoke again until Isaac assisted Melissa out of the chaise at her own gate.

"Good-bye," he said then, shortly.

Melissa looked up at him and caught her breath. She could not speak. Isaac sprang into his chaise, and was out of the yard with a sharp grate of wheels, and she went into the house.

Her mother was setting chairs in order for the evening meeting. She looked up sharply as Melissa entered.

"Who was that brought you home?" said she.

"Isaac Penfield," replied Melissa, turning her face from her mother's eyes.

"I hope you ain't letting your thoughts dwell on anything of that kind now," said her mother.

"I met him as I was coming out of the store, and he asked me to ride. I sha'n't ever see him again," Melissa returned, faintly.

The deaf-and-dumb boy had been dozing with gaping mouth in his chimney-corner. Now he waked, and caught sight of his sister and the basket, and hastened to her with a cry of uncouth hunger and greediness.

"In a minute, sonny," Melissa said, in a sobbing voice; "wait a minute." She held the basket aloof while she removed her hood and shawl.

"You may see him on his way to the outer darkness," said her mother, with solemn vindictiveness.

"Mother, he has repented; he is a member of the church," Melissa cried out, with sudden sharpness.

"Repentance avails nothing without faith," returned her mother, setting down a chair so heavily that the deaf-and-dumb boy started at the concussion and looked about him wonderingly.

"He has repented; he is a member of the church; he is safe," Melissa cried again.

"I tell you he is not," said her mother.

Melissa went into the pantry with her brother at her elbow, and prepared for him a plate of bread and molasses. The tears fell over her cheeks, but Alonzo noticed nothing. His greedy eyes were fixed on the food. When it was ready for him he sat down on his stool in the chimney-corner and devoured it with loud smacks of his lips. That was all the evening meal prepared in the Lennox house that night. After the chairs were set in order for the meeting, Melissa and her mother sat down close to the fire and sewed on some white stuff which flowed in voluminous folds over their knees to the floor. Solomon came in presently, and seated himself with the great Bible on his knees. He read silently, but now and then gesticulated fiercely, as if he read aloud.

The meeting began at half-past six. About a quarter of an hour before, the outer door was heard opening, and there was a shuffling step and a clearing cough in the entry.

"It's your uncle Simeon," whispered Mrs. Lennox to Melissa, and her mouth took on a severer tension.

Solomon frowned over the Holy Writ on his knee.

Simeon advanced into the room, his heavy boots clapping the floor with a dull clatter as of wood, dispelling the solemn stillness. His grinning old face, blue with the cold, was sunk in the collar of his great-coat. He rubbed his hands together as he approached the fire.

"Well, how are ye all?" he remarked, with a chuckle, as if there were a joke in the speech.

Nobody replied. Simeon pulled a chair up close to the fire and sat down.

"It's tarnal cold," said he, leaning over and spreading out his old hands to the blaze.

"The brands are all ready for the burning," said his sister-in-law, in a hollow, trembling voice. She drew a long thread through the white stuff on her knee.

Simeon turned suddenly and looked at her with a flash of small bright eyes. Then he laughed. "Lord bless ye, Sophy Anne, I forgot how tarnal hot you folks are calculatin' to have it day after to-morrow," said he. "Well, if you fail in your calculations, an' the cold continues, I shall be mighty glad to come in here. My house is darned cold this weather, and Abby Mosely ain't particular 'bout the doors; seems to me sometimes as if I was settin' in a hurricane the heft of the time,

and as if my idees were gettin' on a slant. Abby
thinks she's goin' up Thursday, and I wish in
thunder she would. I wouldn't have her another
day, if she wa'n't a lone woman and nowheres to
go. She ain't no kind of a cook. Look at here,
Sophy Anne—"

Mrs. Lennox sewed on with compressed lips.

"Sophy Anne, look at here. You 'ain't got no
mince-pies on hand now, have you?"

"No, I 'ain't."

"Well, I didn't much s'pose you'd made any,
you've been so busy gettin' ready to fly lately.
Look at here, Sophy Anne, don't you feel as if
you could roll me out a few mince-pies to-morrow,
hey?"

Mrs. Lennox looked at him.

"I dun'no' when I've eat a decent mince-pie,"
pursued Simeon. "Abby Mosely keeps the com-
mandments, but she can't make pies that's fit to
eat. I 'ain't had a mince-pie I could eat since my
last wife died. I wish you'd contrive an' roll me
out a few, Sophy Anne. Your mince-pies used
to go ahead of Maria's; she always said they did.
If the world don't come to an end day after to-
morrow, I'd take a sight of comfort with 'em, and
I'll be darned, if it does come to an end, if I don't
think I'd have a chance to eat one or two of 'em
before the fire got round to me. Can't ye do it,
Sophy Anne, nohow?"

"No, I can't."

"Can't ye roll me out just half a dozen mince-pies?"

"I will never roll out a mince-pie for you, Simeon Lennox," said Sophia Anne, with icy fervor.

"Ye never will?"

"No, I never will." Sophia Anne's stern eyes in their hollow blue orbits met his.

Simeon chuckled; then he turned to his brother. "Well, Sol'mon, s'pose you're flappin' all ready to fly?" he said.

Solomon made no reply. He frowned over the great volume on his knees. The deaf-and-dumb boy had set his empty plate on the hearth and fallen asleep again, with his head tilted against the jamb. Melissa sewed, her pale face bent closely over her work.

"Hear ye are goin' to fly from Penfield's hill?" said Simeon.

Still Solomon said nothing.

"Well, I s'pose that's as good a place as any," said Simeon, "though 'tain't a very high hill. I should 'most think you'd want a higher hill than Penfield's. I s'pose you'll be kind of unhandy with your wings at first, an' start off something like hens. But then I s'pose a few feet more or less won't make no odds when they get fairly to workin'. I heard the women was makin' flyin'-petticoats. Them what you're to work on, Sophy Anne, you and Melissy?"

Sophia Anne gave one look at him, then she took a stitch.

"Abby Mosely's to work on one, I guess," said Simeon. "She's ben a-settin' in a heap of white cloth a-sewin' for three days. I came in once, an' she was tryin' of it on, an' she slipped out of it mighty sudden. All I've got to say is she'll cut a queer figure flyin'. She's pretty hefty. I miss my guess if she don't find it a job to strike out at first. Now I should think you might take to flyin' pretty natural, Sophy Anne."

Mrs. Lennox's pale face was flushed with anger, but she sewed on steadily.

"As for Melissy," said Simeon, in his chuckling drawl, "I rather guess she could fly without much practice too. She's built light; but it strikes me she'd better have a weddin'-gown than a flyin'-petticoat. Young Penfield goin' to fly with you, Melissy?"

Solomon Lennox closed the Bible with a great clap. "I'll have no more of this!" he said, with a shout of long-repressed fury.

"Now, Solomon, don't ye get riled so near the end of the world," drawled his brother, getting up slowly. "I'm a-goin'. I ain't goin' to be the means of makin' you backslide when ye're so nigh the top of Zion's Hill. I'm a-goin' home. I don't s'pose I shall get no supper on account of Abby's hurryin' up on her flyin'-petticoat. Sure you ain't goin' to make them mince-pies for me, Sophy Anne?"

"Yes, I be sure."

The brother-in-law thrust his sharp old face down close to Sophia Anne's. "Sure?" he repeated.

Sophia Anne started back and stared at him. There was something strange in his manner.

The old man laughed, and straightened himself. "Well, I'm a-goin'," said he. "Good-bye. Mebbe I sha'n't see ye again before ye fly. Hope ye'll light easy. Good-bye."

After Simeon had closed the door, he opened it again, and thrust his sharp features through a narrow aperture. "Look at here, Solomon," said he. "Mind ye leave the key in the door when ye go out to fly Thursday night. I want to come right in." Then Simeon shut the door again, but his malicious laugh could be plainly heard in the entry.

He did not go straight home as he had said, but up the road to Lawyer Bascombe's office. When he returned, the meeting in his brother's house was in session, and the windows were dark with heads against the red firelight. Old Simeon stared up at them, and laughed aloud to himself as he went by. "Sophy Anne won't make me no mince-pies. She's sure on't," he said, and laughed again.

The next day all the ordinary routine of life

215

seemed at a standstill in the village. The store-
keeper had become a convert, the store was closed,
and the green inside shutters were fastened. Now
and then a village loafer lounged disconsolately
up, shook the door on its rattling lock, stared at
the shuttered windows, then lounged away, muttering. The summer resting-place of his kind,
the long, bewhittled wooden bench on the store
platform, could not be occupied that wintry day.
The air was clear, and the dry pastures were white
and stiff with the hoar-frost; the slants of the
roofs glistened with it in the sun. The breaths
of the people going to and from Solomon Lennox's house were like white smoke. The meeting began at dawn. Children were dragged hither
at their parents' heels, cold and breakfastless.
Not a meal was cooked that day in the houses of
Solomon Lennox's followers. All the precious
hours were spent in fasting and prayer. Towards
night the excitement deepened. There was present within the village a spiritual convulsion as
real as any other convulsion of nature, and as
truly although more subtly felt. Even they who
had scoffed and laughed at this new movement
from the first, and were now practically untouched
by it, grew nervous and ill at ease towards night
as from the gathering of a storm. The air seemed
charged with electricity generated by the touch
of human thought and faith with the Unknown.
The unbelievers pressed their faces against the

window-panes, shading their eyes from the light within as the dusk deepened, or stood out in their yards watching the sky, half fearful they should indeed see some sign or marvel therein.

But the night came on, and the stars shone out in their order as they had done from the first, and there was no sign but the old one of eternal love and beauty in the sky. The moon arose at nine o'clock, nearly at her full. That, from some interpretation of symbolical characters on the deaf-and-dumb boy's slate, had been fixed upon as the hour of meeting upon Penfield's hill. The solemn and dreadful moment which was to mark the climax of all creation was expected between that hour and dawn.

At half-past eight white-robed figures began to move along the road. People peeped around their curtains to see them pass; now and then belated children ran shrieking with terror into the houses at sight of them.

Beside the road, close to the gate which led to the wide field at the foot of Penfield's hill, under the shadow of a clump of hemlocks, Isaac Penfield had been waiting since quarter past eight o'clock. When the white company came in sight he drew farther back within the shadow, scanning the people eagerly as they passed.

Solomon Lennox and Deacon Scranton let down the bars, and the people passed through silently, crowding each other whitely like a flock of sheep. Sophia Anne, the deaf-and-dumb boy holding fast to her hand, was among the first.

Isaac had expected to see Melissa close to her mother ; but she had become separated from her and came among the last.

Her slender figure was hidden in her flowing white robes, but there was no mistaking her gentle faltering gait and the delicate bend of her fair uncovered head.

Isaac stepped forward suddenly, threw his arm around Melissa, and drew her back with him within the shadow of the hemlocks. Nobody saw it but Abby Mosely, Simeon Lennox's housekeeper, and she was too panic-stricken to heed it intelligently ; she went panting on after the others in her voluminous white robe, and left Melissa alone with Isaac Penfield.

Isaac pressed Melissa's head close to his breast, leaned his face down to hers, and whispered long in her ear. She listened trembling and unresisting ; then she broke away from him weakly, "I can't, I can't," she moaned. But he caught her again, and whispered again with his lips close to her soft pale cheek, and frequent kisses between the words.

"Come, now, sweetheart," he said at length, and attempted to draw her with him into the road ; but she pulled herself away from him again, and stood warding him off with her white-draped arms.

"I can't, I can't," she moaned again. "I must go with father and mother."

"I tell you they are wrong; can't you believe me?"

"I—must—go with them."

"No; come with me, Melissa."

Melissa, still with her arms raised against him, looked away over the meadow, full of moving white figures. The moon shone out over it, and it gleamed like a field of Paradise peopled with angels. Then she looked up in her lover's face, and suddenly it was to her as if she saw therein the new earth of all her dreams.

Solomon Lennox and his followers kept on to Penfield's hill, which arose before them crowned with silver, and Isaac Penfield hastened down the road to the village, half carrying Melissa's little white-clad figure, wrapped against the cold in his own gray cloak.

Early the next morning a small company of pallid shivering people crept through the village to their homes. Many had weakened and deserted long before dawn, chilled to their very thoughts and fancies by their long vigil on the hill-top. Young girls ran home, crying aloud like children, and men half dragged hysterical wives rigid with chills. Solomon Lennox and his wife remained until the dawn light shone; then he beckoned to her and the whimpering deaf-and-dumb boy, and led the way down the hill without a word. He never looked at the rest of the company, but they followed silently.

The Penfield house was about a quarter of a mile from the pasture bars. When they reached it, Isaac stood waiting at the gate. He went up to Solomon, who was passing without a look, and touched his arm with an impatient yet respectful gesture. "You and Mrs. Lennox and Lonny had better come in here, I think," he said.

Solomon was moving on with dull obstinacy, but Isaac laid his hand on his arm. "I—think you have—forgotten," he said. "I am sorry, but —your brother Simeon has—taken possession of your house."

Solomon stared at him dully. He did not seem to comprehend. Sophia Anne looked as blue and bloodless in her white robe as if she were dead. She had scarce more control of her trembling tongue than if it were paralyzed, but her highly strung feminine nerves gave out vibrations still.

"Has Simeon took possession?" she demanded, fiercely.

Isaac Penfield nodded. "I think it would be pleasanter for you to come in here now," he said. Then he hesitated, and colored suddenly. "Your daughter is in here," he added.

Sophia Anne gave a keen glance at him. Then she turned in at the gate with a sharp twitch at the arm of the deaf-and-dumb boy, who was making strange cries and moans, like a distressed animal. "Come, father," she called, impatiently; and Solomon also entered the Penfield gate with a piteous, dazed air.

In the great south room of the Penfield house were Melissa and Mrs. Martha Joyce, the housekeeper. Mrs. Joyce was mixing something in a steaming bowl; Melissa sat still, gazing at the fire. She was dressed in a blue satin gown and fine lace tucker, which had belonged to Isaac Penfield's mother. Madam Penfield had been nearly Melissa's size, and the gown fitted her slender figure daintily. She sat with her fair head bent, the color coming and going in her soft cheeks, as if from her own thoughts. Her little hands were folded in her blue satin lap, and on one finger gleamed a great pearl, which Madam Penfield had used to wear.

When the door opened and her parents entered, she half started up, with a great blush; then she sank back, trembling and pale.

Isaac Penfield crossed over to her, and laid his hand on her shoulder. "She is my wife," he said. "We were married last night."

Sophia Anne made a faint gesture, which might have expressed anything. Solomon staggered to a chair without a look. In truth, when they entered the warm room, and the long strain of resistance against cold and fatigue ceased, exhaustion overcame them. Mrs. Joyce administered hot porridge and cordials, and Melissa knelt down in her blue satin and rubbed her mother's benumbed hands.

Solomon took whatever was offered him, meekly, like a child. His face was changed; the look which it had worn during the greater part of his life, the expression of himself within his old worn channel, had returned.

He was sitting by the fire, sipping cordial, when his brother Simeon came in; he had not even noticed the brazen clang of the knocker.

Simeon came tiptoeing around in front of his brother, thrust down his face on a level with his, and peered at him with a sharp twinkle of black eyes. Then he looked at Sophia Anne, and chuckled. "'Pears to me wings didn't work very well," said he.

Simeon had a roll of paper in his hand. He went to the desk, and spread it out ostentatiously. Then he began to read in a high, solemn voice, with an undertone of merriment in it. "Know all men by these presents," began Simeon Lennox, and read straight through the deed, with all its strange legal formalities, by which his brother Solomon had conveyed his worldly goods to him.

Sophia Anne writhed in her chair as Simeon read. She was on a rack of torture, and every new word was a turn of the screw. Solomon set his tumbler of cordial on the hearth, and rested his head on his hands.

After Simeon had finished reading the deed, he paused for a moment. Sophia Anne gave a dry sob.

Then Simeon cleared his throat, and continued: "The foregoing I do hereby declare null and void, and I do hereby remise, release, sell, and forever quitclaim, for myself and my heirs, by these presents, the aforementioned premises, with all the privileges and appurtenances thereunto belonging, to the said Solomon Lennon, his heirs and assigns forever, in consideration that Sophia Anne, the wife of said Solomon Lennox, shall, during the term of her natural life, unless she be prevented by sickness from so doing, make, mix, season, and bake for me with her own hands, with her best skill, according to her own conscience, seven mince pies during every week of the year, with one extra for every Independence and Thanksgiving day, and that the said Sophia Anne, the wife of the said Solomon Lennox, shall hereunto set her hand and seal."

Simeon looked at Sophia Anne. She stared back at him, speechless.

"Well, what ye goin' to do about it, Sophy Anne?" said Simeon.

Sophia Anne still looked at him as if he were a blank wall against which her very spirit had been brought to a standstill.

" Goin' to sign it, Sophy Anne ?"

Sophia Anne got up. Her knees trembled, but she motioned back Isaac Penfield's proffered arm. She went to the desk, sat down, took the quill, dipped it carefully in the inkstand, and shook it lest it blot. Her lean arm crooked as stiffly as a stick, her lips were a blue line, but she wrote her name with sharply rippling strokes, and laid the pen down.

" Sure ye won't make them mince pies, Sophy Anne ?" said Simeon.

Sophia Anne made no reply. She put her elbow on the desk, and leaned her head on her hand. Simeon looked at her a moment, then he gave her a rough pat on her shoulder and turned and went to the window, and stood there, staring out.

Melissa was weeping softly ; Isaac stood beside her, smoothing her hair tenderly. The deaf-and-dumb boy's fair head hung helplessly over his shoulder. He had fallen asleep with the tears on his cheeks.

The morning sunlight shone broadly into the room over them all, but Solomon Lennox did not seem to heed that or anything that was around him, sitting sadly within himself : a prophet brooding over the ashes of his own prophetic fire.

THE LITTLE MAID AT THE DOOR

JOSEPH BAYLEY and his wife Ann came riding down from Salem village. They had started from their home in Newbury the day before, and had stayed overnight with their relative, Sergeant Thomas Putnam, in Salem village; they were on their way to the election in Boston. The road wound along through the woods from Salem to Lynn; it was some time since they had passed a house.

May was nearly gone; the pinks and the black-berry vines were in flower. All the woods were full of an indefinite and composite fragrance, made up of the breaths of myriads of green plants and seen and unseen blossoms, like a very bou-quet of spring. The newly leaved trees cast shad-ows that were as much a part of the tender sur-prise of the spring as the new flowers. They flickered delicately before Joseph Bayley and his wife Ann on the grassy ridges of the road, but they did not remark them. Their own fancies

cast gigantic projections which eclipsed the sweet
show of the spring and almost their own person-
alities. That year the leaves came out and the
flowers bloomed in vain for the people in and
about Salem village. There was epidemic a dis-
ease of the mind which deafened and blinded to
all save its own pains.

Ann Bayley on the pillion snuggled closely
against her husband's back; her fearful eyes
peered at the road around his shoulder. She was
a young and handsome woman; she had on her
best mantle of sad-colored silk, and a fine black
hood with a topknot, but she did not think of that.

"Joseph, what is that in the road before us?"
she whispered, timorously.

He pulled up the horse with a great jerk.
"Where?" he whispered back.

"There! there! at the right; just beyond that
laurel thicket. 'Tis somewhat black, an' it moves.
There! there! Oh, Joseph!"

Joseph Bayley sat stiff and straight in his saddle, like a soldier; his face was pale and stern,
his eyes full of horror and defiance.

"See you it?" Ann whispered again. "There!
now it moves. What is it?"

"I see it," said Joseph, in a loud, bold voice.
"An' whatever it be, I will yield not to it; an'
neither will you, goodwife."

Ann reached around and caught at the reins.
"Let us go back," she moaned, faintly. "Oh,

Joseph, let us not pass it. My spirit faints within me. I see its back among the laurel blooms. 'Tis the black beast they tell of. Let us turn back, Joseph, let us turn back!"

"Be still, woman!" returned her husband, jerking the reins from her hand. "What think ye 'twould profit us to turn back to Salem village? I trow if there be one black beast here, there is a full herd of them there. There is naught left but to ride past it as best we may. Sit fast, an' listen you not to it, whatever it promise you." Joseph looked down the road towards the laurel bushes, his muscles now as tense as a bow. Ann hid her face on his shoulder. Suddenly he shouted, with a great voice like a herald : "Away with ye, ye cursed beast! away with ye ! We are not of your kind ; we are gospel folk. We have naught to do with you or your master. Away with ye !"

The horse leaped forward. There was a great cracking among the laurel bushes at the right, a glossy black back and some white horns heaved over them, then some black flanks plunged heavily out of sight.

" Oh !" shrieked Ann, "has it gone ? Goodman, has it gone ?"

" The Lord hath delivered us from the snare of the enemy," answered Joseph, solemnly.

" What looked it like, Joseph, what looked it like ?"

"Like no beast that was saved in the ark."

"Had it fiery eyes?" asked Ann, trembling.

"'Tis well you did not see them."

"Ride fast! oh, ride fast!" Ann pleaded, clutching hard at her husband's cloak. "It may follow on our track." The horse went down the road at a quick trot. Ann kept peering back and starting at every sound in the woods. "Do you mind the tale Samuel Endicott told last night?" she said, shuddering. "How on his voyage to Barbadoes he, sitting on the windlass on a bright moonshining night, was shook violently, and saw the appearance of that witch Goody Bradbury, with a white cap and a white neckcloth on her? It was a dreadful tale."

"It was naught to the sight of Mercy Lewis and Sergeant Thomas Putnam's daughter Ann, when they were set upon and nigh choked to death by Goody Proctor. Know you that within a half-mile we must pass the Proctor house?"

Ann gave a shuddering sigh. "I would I were home again!" she moaned. "They said 'twas full of evil things, and that the black man himself kept tavern there since Goodman Proctor and his wife were in jail. Did you mind what Goodwife Putnam said of the black head, like a hog's, that Goodman Perley saw at the keeping-room window as he passed, and the rumbling noises, and the yellow birds that flew around the chimney and twittered in a psalm tune? Oh, Joseph, there is a yellow bird now in the birch-tree—see! see!"

They had come into a little space where the woods were thinner. Joseph urged his horse forward.

"We will not slack our pace for any black beasts nor any yellow birds," he cried, in a valiant voice.

There was a passing gleam of little yellow wings above the birch-tree.

"He has flown away," said Ann. "'Tis best to front them as you do, goodman, but I have not the courage. That looked like a common yellowbird; his wings shone like gold. Think you it has gone forward to the Proctor house?"

"It matters not, so it but fly up before us," said Joseph Bayley.

He was somewhat older than Ann; fair-haired and fair-bearded, with blue eyes set so deeply under heavy brows that they looked black. His face was at once stern and nervous, showing not only the spirit of warfare against his foes, but the elements of strife within himself.

They rode on, and the woods grew thicker; the horse's hoofs made only a faint liquid pad on the mossy road. Suddenly he stopped and whinnied. Ann clutched her husband's arm; they sat motionless, listening; the horse whinnied again.

Suddenly Joseph started violently, and stared

into the woods on the left, and Ann also. A long
defile of dark evergreens stretched up the hill,
with mysterious depths of blue-black shadows between them ; the air had an earthy dampness.

Joseph shook the reins fiercely over the horse's
back, and shouted to him in a loud voice.

"Did you see it ?" gasped Ann, when they
had come into a lighter place. "Was it not a
black man ?"

"Fear not; we have outridden him," said her
husband, setting his thin intense face proudly
ahead.

"I would we were safe home in Newbury,"
Ann moaned. "I would we had never set out.
Think you not Dr. Mather will ride back from
Boston with us to keep the witches off ? I will
bide there forever, if he will not. I will never
come this dreadful road again, else. What is
that ? Oh, what is that ? 'Tis a voice coming
out of the woods like a great roar. *Joseph!* What
is *that?* That was a black cat run across the road
into the bushes. 'Twas a black cat. Joseph, let
us turn back ! No ; the black man is behind us,
and the beast. What shall we do ? What shall
we do ? Oh, oh, I begin to twitch like Ann and
Mercy last night ! My feet move, and I cannot
stop them ! Now there is a pin thrust in my
arm ! I am pinched ! There are fingers at my
throat ! Joseph ! Joseph !"

"Go to prayer, sweetheart," shouted Joseph.

"Go to prayer. Be not afraid. 'Twill drive them away. Away with ye, Goody Bradbury! Away, Goody Proctor! Go to prayer, go to prayer!"

Joseph bent low in the saddle and lashed the horse, which sprang forward with a mighty bound; the green branches rushed in their faces. Joseph prayed in a loud voice. Ann clung to him convulsively, panting for breath. Suddenly they came out of the woods into a cleared space.

"The Proctor house! the Proctor house!" Ann shrieked. "Mercy Lewis said 'twas full of devils. What shall we do?" She hid her face on her husband's shoulder, sobbing and praying.

The Proctor house stood at the left of the road; there were some peach-trees in front of it, and their blossoms showed in a pink spray against the gray unpainted walls. On one side of the house was the great barn, with its doors wide open; on the other, a deep ploughed field, with the plough sticking in a furrow. John Proctor had been arrested and thrown into jail for witchcraft in April, before his spring planting was done.

Joseph Bayley reined in his horse opposite the Proctor house. "Ann," he whispered, and his whisper was full of horror.

"What is it?" she returned, wildly.

"Ann, Goodman Proctor looks forth from the chamber window, and Goody Proctor stands outside by the well, and they are both in jail in Boston." Joseph's whole frame shook in a strange rigid fashion, as if his joints were locked. "Look, Ann!" he whispered.

"I cannot."

"Look!"

Ann turned her head. "Why," she said, and her voice was quite natural and sweet, it had even a tone of glad relief in it, "I see naught but a little maid in the door."

"See you not Goodman Proctor in the window?"

"Nay," said Ann, smiling; "I see naught but the little maid in the door. She is in a blue petticoat, and she has a yellow head, but her little cheeks are pale, I trow."

"See you not Goodwife Proctor in the yard by the well?" asked Joseph.

"Nay, goodman; I see naught but the little maid in the door. She has a fair face, but now she falls a-weeping. Oh, I fear lest she be all alone in the house."

"I tell you, Goodman Proctor and Goodwife Proctor are both there," returned Joseph. "Think you I see not with my own eyes? Goodman Proctor has on a red cap, and Goodwife Proctor holds a spindle." He urged on the horse with a sudden cry. "Now the prayers do stick in my throat," he groaned. "I would we were out of this devil's nest!"

"Oh, Joseph," implored Ann, "prithee wait

"'I SEE NAUGHT BUT A LITTLE MAID IN THE DOOR'"

a minute! The little maid is calling 'mother' after me. Saw you not how she favored our little Susanna who died? Hear her! There was naught there but the little maid. Joseph, I pray you, stop."

"Nay; I'll ride till the nag drops," said Joseph Bayley, with a lash. "This last be too much. I tell ye they are there, and they are also in jail. 'Tis hellish work."

Ann said no more for a little space; a curve in the road hid the Proctor house from sight. Suddenly she raised a great cry. "Oh! oh!" she screamed, "'tis gone : 'tis gone from my foot!"

Joseph stopped. "What is gone?"

"My shoe; but now I missed it from my foot. I must alight, and go back for it."

Joseph started the horse again.

Ann caught at the reins. "Stop, goodman," she cried, imperatively. "I tell you I must have my shoe."

"And I tell you I'll stop for no shoe in this place, were it made of gold."

"Goodman, you know not what shoe 'tis. 'Tis one of my fine shoes, in which I have never taken steps. They have the crimson silk lacings. I have even carried them in my hand to the meeting-house on a Sabbath, wearing my old ones, and only put them on at the door. Think you I will lose that shoe? Stop the nag."

But Joseph kept on grimly.

"Think you I will go barefoot or with one shoe into Boston?" said Ann. "Know you that these shoes, which were a present from my mother, cost bravely? I trow you will needs loosen your purse strings well before we pass the first shop in Boston. Well, go on, an' you will, when 'tis but a matter of my slipping down from the pillion and running back a few yards."

Joseph Bayley turned his horse about; but Ann remonstrated.

"Nay," said she; "I want not to go thus. I am tired of the saddle. I would like to feel my feet for a space."

Her husband looked around at her with wonder and suspicion. Dark thoughts came into his mind.

She laughed. "Nay," said she, "make no such face at me. I go not back to meet any black man nor sign any book. I go for my fine shoe with the crimson lacing."

"'Tis but a moment since you were afraid," said Joseph. "Have you no fear now?" His blue eyes looked sharply into hers.

She looked back at him soberly and innocently. "In truth, I feel no such fear as I did," she answered. "If I mistake not, your bold front and your prayers drove away the evil ones. I will say a psalm as I go, and I trow naught will harm me."

Ann slipped lightly down from the pillion, and

pulled off her one remaining shoe and her stockings; they were her fine worked silk ones, and she could not walk in them over the rough road. Then she set forth very slowly, peering here and there in the undergrowth beside the road, until she passed the curve and the reach of her husband's eyes. Then she gathered up her crimson taffeta petticoat and ran like a deer, with long graceful leaps, looking neither to right nor left, straight back to the Proctor house.

In the door of the house stood a tiny girl with a soft shock of yellow hair. She wore a little straight blue gown, and her baby feet were bare, curling over the sunny door-step. When she saw Ann coming she started as if to run; then she stood still, her soft eyes wary, her mouth quivering.

Ann Bayley ran up quickly, and threw her arms around her, kneeling down on the step. "What is your name, little maid?" said she, in a loving, agitated voice.

"Abigail Proctor," replied the little maid, shyly, in her sweet childish treble. Then she tried to free herself, but Ann held her fast.

"Nay, be not afraid, sweet," said she. "I love you. I once had a little maid like you for my own. Tell me, dear heart, are you all alone in the house?"

Then the child fell to crying again, and clung around Ann's neck.

"Is there anybody in the house, sweet?" Ann whispered, fondling her, and pressing the wet baby cheek to her own.

"The constables came and took them," sobbed the little maid. "They put my poppet down the well, and they pulled mother and Sarah down the road. They took father before that, and Mary Warren did gibe and point. The constables pulled Benjamin away too. I want my mother."

"Your mother shall come again," said Ann. "Take comfort, dear little heart, they cannot have the will to keep her long away. There, there, I tell you she shall come. You watch in the door, and you will see her come down the road."

She smoothed back the little maid's yellow hair, and wiped the tears from her little face with a corner of her beautiful embroidered neckerchief. Then she saw that the face was all grimy with tears and dust, and she went over to the well, which was near the door, and drew a bucket of water swiftly with her strong young arms; then she wet the corner of the neckerchief and scrubbed the little maid's face, bidding her shut her eyes. Then she kissed her over and over.

"Now you are sweet and clean," said she. "Dear little heart, I have some sugar cakes in my bag for you, and then I must be gone."

The little maid looked at her eagerly, her cheeks were waxen, and the blue veins showed in her full childish forehead. Ann pulled some little cakes out of a red velvet satchel she wore at her waist, and Abigail reached out for one with a hungry cry. The tears sprang to Ann's eyes; she put the rest of the cakes in a little pile on the door-stone, and watched the child eat. Then she gathered her up in her arms.

"Good-bye, sweetheart," she said, kissing the soft trembling mouth, the sweet hollow under the chin, and the clinging hands. "Before long I shall come this way again, and do you stand in the door when I go past."

She put her down and hastened away, but little Abigail ran after her. Ann stopped and knelt and fondled her again.

"Go back, deary," she pleaded; "go back, and eat the sugar cakes."

But this beautiful kind vision in the crimson taffeta, with the rosy cheeks and sweet black eyes looking out from the French hood, with the gleam of gold and delicate embroidery between the silken folds of her mantilla, with the ways like her mother's, was more to little deserted Abigail Proctor than the sugar cakes, although she was sorely hungry for them. She stood aloof with pitiful determined eyes until Ann's back was turned, then, as she followed, Ann looked around and saw her and caught her up again.

"My dear heart, my dear heart," she said, and she was half sobbing, "now must you go back, else I fear harm will come to you. My goodman is waiting for me yonder, and I know not what he will do or say. Nay; you must go back. I would I could keep you, my little Abigail, but you must go back." Ann Bayley put the little maid down and gave her a gentle push. "Go back," she said, smiling, with her eyes full of tears; "go back, and eat the sugar cakes."

Then she sped on swiftly; as she neared the curve in the road she thrust a hand in her pocket, and drew forth a dainty shoe with dangling lacings of crimson silk. She glanced around with a smile and a backward wave of her hand; the glowing crimson of her petticoat showed for a minute through the green mist of the undergrowth; then she disappeared.

The little maid Abigail stood still in the road, gazing after her, her soft pink mouth open, her hands clutching at her blue petticoat, as if she would thus hold herself back from following. She heard the tramp of a horse's feet beyond the curve; then it died away. She turned about and went back to the house, with the tears rolling over her cheeks; but she did not sob aloud, as she would have done had her mother been near to hear. A pitiful conviction of the hopelessness of all the appeals of grief was stealing over her childish mind. She had been alone in the house

three nights and two days, ever since her sister
Sarah and her brother Benjamin had been arrested for witchcraft and carried to jail. Long
before that her parents, John and Elizabeth
Proctor, had disappeared down the Boston road
in charge of the constables. None of the family
was spared save this little Abigail, who was
deemed too young and insignificant to have deal-
ings with Satan, and was therefore not thrown
into prison, but was left alone in the desolate
Proctor house in the midst of woods said to be
full of evil spirits and witches, to die of fright or
starvation as she might. There was but little
mercy shown the families of those accused of
witchcraft.

"Let some of Goody Proctor's familiars minister unto the brat," one of the constables had
said, with a stern laugh, when Abigail had followed wailing after her brother and sister on the
day of their arrest.

"Yea," said another; "she can send her yel-
low-bird or her black hog to keep her company.
I wot her tears will be soon dried."

Then the stoutly tramping horses had borne
out of sight and hearing the mocking faces of the
constables; Sarah's fair agonized one turned
backward towards her little deserted sister, and
Benjamin raised a brave youthful clamor of indignation.

"Let us loose!" Abigail heard him shout; "let

us loose, I tell ye! Ye are fools, rather than we are witches; ye are fools and murderers! Let us loose, I tell ye!"

Abigail waited long, thinking her brother's words would prevail; but neither he nor Sarah returned, and the sounds all died away, and she went back to the house sobbing. The damp spring night was settling down in a palpable mist, and the woods seemed full of voices. The little maid had heard enough of the terrible talk of the day to fill her innocent head with vague superstitious horror. She threw her apron over her head and fled blindly through the woods, and now and then she fell down and bruised herself, and rose up lamenting sorely, with nobody to hear her.

As soon as she was in the house she shut the doors, and barred them with the great bars that had been made as protection against Indians, and now might wax useless against worse than savages, according to the belief of the colony.

All night long the little maid shrieked and sobbed, and called on her father and her mother and her sister and her brother. Men faring in the road betwixt Boston and Salem village heard her with horror, and fled past with psalm and prayer, their blood cold in their veins. They related the next day to the raging, terror-stricken people how at midnight the accursed Proctor house was full of flitting infernal lights, and howling with devilish spirits, and added a death-dealing tale of some godly woman of the village who outrode their horses on a broomstick and disappeared in the Proctor house.

The next day the little maid unbarred the door, and stood there watching up and down the road for her mother or some other to come. But they came not, although she watched all day. That night she did not sob and call out; she had become afraid of her own voice, and discovered that it had no effect to bring her help. Then, too, early in the night, she heard noises about the house which frightened her, and made her think that perchance the dreadful black beast of which she had heard them discourse was abroad.

The next morning she found that the two horses and the cow and calf were gone from the barn; also that there was left scarce anything for her to eat in the house. There had been some loaves of bread, some boiled meat, and some cakes; now they were all gone, and also all the meal from the chest, and the potatoes and pork from the cellar. But for that last she did not care, since she was not old enough to make a fire and cook. She had left for food only a little cold porridge in a blue bowl, and that she ate up at once and had no more, and a little buttermilk in a crock, which, she being not over-fond of it, served her longer. But that was all she had had for a day and a night, until Goodwife Ann Bayley gave

Q   241

her the sugar cakes. These she ate up at once
on her return to the house. Then again she
stood watching in the door, but nothing passed
along the road save a partridge or a squirrel. It
was accounted a bold thing for any solitary trav-
eller to come this way, save a witch, and she, it
was supposed, might find many comrades in the
woods beside the road and in the Proctor house,
which was held to be a sort of devils' tavern. But
now no witch came, nor any of her uncanny
friends, unless indeed the squirrel and the partridge were familiar demons in disguise. Nothing was too harmless and simple to escape that
imputation of the devil's mask.

Abigail took her little pewter porringer from
the cupboard, and got herself a drink of water
from the bucketful that Goodwife Bayley had
drawn; then she stood on a stone, and peered
into the well, leaning over the curb. Her poppet was in there, her dear rag doll that Sarah had
made for her, and dressed in a beautiful silver
brocade made from a piece of a wedding-gown
that was brought from England. One of the
constables had caught sight of little Abigail Proctor's poppet, and being straightway filled with
suspicion that it was an image whereby Goody
Proctor afflicted her victims by proxy, had seized
it and thrown it into the well. The other constables had chidden him for such rashness, saying it should have been carried to Boston and

produced as evidence at the trial; and little Abigail had shrieked out in a panic for her poppet.

She could see nothing of it now, and she went back to her watching-place in the door.

In the afternoon she felt sorely hungry again, and searched through the house for food; then she went out in the sunny fields behind the house, and found some honeysuckles on the rocks, and sucked the honey greedily from their horns. On her return to the house she found a corn-cob, which she snatched up and folded in her apron, and began tending. She sat down in the doorway in her little chair, which she dragged out of the keeping-room, and hugged the poor poppet close, and crooned over it.

"Be not afraid," said she. "I'll not let the black beast harm you; I promise you I will not."

That night she formed a new plan for her solace and protection in the lonely darkness. All the garments of her lost parents and sister and brother that she could find she gathered together, and formed in a circle on the keeping-room floor; then she crept inside with her corn-cob poppet, and lay there hugging it all night. The next day she watched again in the door; but now she was weak and faint, and her little legs trembled so under her that she could not stand to watch, but sat in her small straight-backed chair, holding her poppet and peering forth wistfully.

In the course of the day she made shift to

creep out into the fields again, and lying flat on the sun‑heated rocks, she sucked some more honey drops from the honeysuckles. She found, too, on the edge of the woods, some young wintergreen leaves, and she even pulled some blue violets and ate them. But the delicate, sweet, and aromatic fare in the spring larder of nature was poor nourishment for a human baby.

Poor little Abigail Proctor could scarcely creep home, still clinging fast to her poppet; scarcely lift herself into her chair in the door; scarcely crawl inside her fairy‑ring of her loved ones' belongings at night. She rolled herself tightly in an old cloak of her father's, and it was a sweet and harmless outcome of the dreadful superstition of the day, grafted on an innocent childish brain, that it seemed to partake of the bodily presence of her father, and protect her.

All night long, as she lay there, her mother cooked good meat and broth and sweet cakes, and she ate her fill of them; but in the morning she was too weak to turn her little body over. She could not get to her watching‑place in the door, but that made no difference to her, for she did not fairly know that she was not there. It seemed to her that she sat in her little chair looking up the road and down the road; she saw the green branches weaving together, and hiding the sky to the northward and the southward; she saw the flushes of white and rose in the flowering undergrowth; she saw the people coming and going. There were her father and mother now coming with store of food and presents for her, now following the constables out of sight. There was that fine pageant passing, as she had seen it pass once before, of the two magistrates, their worshipful masters John Hathorne and Jonathan Corwin, with the marshal, constables, and aids, splendid and awe-inspiring in all their trappings of office, to examine the accused in the Salem meeting-house. There were the ministers Parris and Noyes coming, with severe malignant faces, to question her mother as to whether she had afflicted Mary Warren, their former maid-servant, who was now bewitched. There went Benjamin, clamoring out boldly at his captors. There came Sarah with the poppet, which she had drawn out of the well, shaking the water from its silver brocade.

All this the little maid Abigail Proctor saw through her half-delirious fancy as she lay weakly on the keeping-room floor, but she saw not the reality of her sister Sarah coming about four o'clock in the afternoon.

Sarah Proctor, tall and slender, in her limp bedraggled dress, with her fair severe face set in a circle of red shawl, which she had pinned under her chin, came resolutely down the road from Boston, driving a black cow before her with a great green branch. She was nearly fainting

with weariness, but she set her dusty shoes down
swiftly among the road weeds, and her face was
as unyielding as an Indian's.

When she came in sight of the Proctor house
she stopped a second. "Abigail!" she called;
"Abigail!"

There was no answer, and she went on more
swiftly than before. When she reached the
house she called again, "Abigail!" but did not
wait except while she tied the black cow, by a
rope which was around her neck, to a peach-tree.
Then she ran in, and found the little maid, her
sister Abigail, on the floor in the keeping-room.

She got down on her knees beside her, and
Abigail smiled up in her face waveringly. She
still thought herself in the door, and that she had
just seen her sister come down the road.

"Abigail, what have they done to you?" asked
Sarah, in a sharp voice; and the little maid only
smiled.

"Abigail, Abigail, what is it?" Sarah took
hold of the child's shoulders and shook her; but
she got no word back, only the smile ceased, and
the eyelids drooped faintly.

"Are you hungry, Abigail?"

The little maid shook her head softly.

"It cannot be that," said Sarah, as if half to
herself; "there was enough in the house; but
what is it? Abigail, look at me; how long is it
since you have eaten? Abigail!"

"Yesterday," whispered the little maid, dreamily.

"What did you eat then?"

"Some posies and leaves out in the field."

"What became of all the bread that was baked, and the cakes, and the meat?"

"I—have forgot."

"No, you have not. Tell me, Abigail."

"The black beast came in the night and did eat it all up, and the cow, and calf, and the horses, too."

"The black beast!"

"I heard him in the night, and in the morning 'twas—gone."

Sarah sprang up. "Robbers and murderers!" she cried, in a fierce voice; but the little maid on the floor did not start; she shut her eyes again, and looked up and down the road.

Sarah got a bucket quickly, and went out in the yard to the cow. Down on her knees in the grass she went and milked; then she carried in the bucket, strained the milk with trembling haste, and poured some into Abigail's little pewter porringer. "She was wont to love it warm," she whispered, with white lips.

She bent close over the little maid, and raised her on one arm, while she put the porringer to her mouth. "Drink, Abigail," she said, with tender command. "'Tis warm—the way you love it."

The little maid tried to sip, but shut her mouth, and turned her head with weak loathing, and Sarah could not compel her. She laid her back, and got a spoon and fed her a little, by dint of much pleading to make her open her mouth and swallow.

Afterwards she undressed her, and put her to bed in the south-front room, but the child was so uneasy without the ring of garments which she had arranged, that Sarah was forced to put them around her on the bed; then she fell asleep directly, and stood in her dream watching in the door.

Sarah herself stood in the door, looking up and down the road. There was the sound of a galloping horse in the distance; it came nearer and nearer. She went down to the road and stood waiting. The horse was reined in close to her, and the young man who rode him sprang off the saddle.

"It is you, Sarah; you are safe home," he cried, eagerly, and would have put his arm about her; but she stood aloof sternly.

"For what else did you take me—my apparition?" she said, in a hard voice.

"Sweetheart!"

"Know you that I have but just come from the jail in Boston, where I have lain fast chained for witchcraft? See you my fine apparel with the prison air in it? Know you that they called

248

me a witch, and said that I did afflict Mary Warren and the rest? I marvel not that you kept
your distance, David Carr; I might perchance
have hurt you, and they might have accused you,
since you were in fellowship with a witch. I
marvel not at that. I would have no harm come
to you, though far greater than this came to me,
but wherefore did you let my little sister Abigail
starve? That can I not suffer, coming from you,
David."

The young man took her in his arms with a de-
cided motion; and indeed she did not repulse
him, but began to weep.

"Sarah," said he, earnestly, "I was in Ipswich. I knew naught of you and Benjamin being cried out upon until within this hour, when
I returned home, and my mother told me. I
knew not you were acquitted, and was on my
way to Boston to you when I saw you at the
gate. And as for Abigail, I knew naught at all;
and so 'twas with my mother, for she but now
wept when she said the poor little maid had been
taken with the rest. But you mean not that,
sweetheart; she has not been let to starve?"

"They stole away the food in the night," said
Sarah, "and the horses and the cow and calf. I
found the cow straying in the woods but now, on
my way home, and drove her in and milked her;
but Abigail would take scarce a spoonful of the
warm milk. She has had but little to eat for

three days, and has been distracted with fear, being left alone. She has ever been but a delicate child, and now I fear she has a fever on her, and will die, with her mother away."

"I will go for my mother, sweetheart," said David Carr, eagerly.

"Bring her under cover of night, then," said Sarah; "else she may be suspected if she come to this witch tavern, as they call it. Oh, David, think you she will come? I am in a sore strait."

"I will bring her without fail, sweet, and a flask of wine also, and needments for the little maid," cried David. "Only do you keep up good heart. Perchance, sweet, the child will amend soon, and the others be soon acquit. Nay, weep not, poor lass! poor lass! Thou hast me, whatever else fail thee, poor solace though that be, and I will fetch thee my mother right speedily. She has ever set great store by the little maid, and knows much about ailments; and I doubt not they will be soon acquit."

"They say my mother will," answered Sarah, tearfully; "and Benjamin is acquit now, but had best keep for a season out of Salem village. But my father will not be acquit; he has spoken his mind too boldly before them all."

"Nay, sweetheart," said David Carr, mounting, "'twill all have passed soon; 'tis but a madness. Go in to the little maid, and be of good comfort."

Sarah went sobbing into the house, but her face was quite calm when she stood over little Abigail. The child was still asleep, and she could arouse her only for a moment to take a few spoonfuls of milk; then she turned her head on her pillow with weary obstinacy, and shut her eyes again. She still held the poor corn-cob poppet fast.

Sarah washed herself, braided her hair, and changed her prison dress for a clean blue linen one; then she sat beside Abigail, and waited for David Carr and his mother, who came within an hour. Goodwife Carr was renowned through Salem village for her knowledge of medicinal herbs and her nursing. She had a gentle sobriety and decision of manner which placed her firmly in her neighbors' confidences, they seeing how she abode firmly in her own, and arguing from that. Then she had too the good fortune to have made no enemies, consequently her ability had not incurred for her the suspicion of being a witch.

Goodwife Carr brought a goodly store of healing herbs, of bread and cakes and meat, and she brewed drinks, and bent her face, pale and soberly faithful, in her close white cap, untiringly over Abigail Proctor. But the little maid never arose again. A fever, engendered by starvation and fright and grief, had seized upon her, and she lay in the bed with her little corn-cob baby a few days longer, and then died.

They made a straight white gown for her, and

dressed her in it, after washing her and smoothing her yellow hair; and she lay, looking longer and older than in life, all set about with flowers —pinks and lilacs and roses—from Goodwife Carr's garden, until she was buried. And they had the Ipswich minister come for the funeral, for David Carr cried out in a fury that Minister Parris, who had prosecuted this witchcraft business, was her murderer, and blood would flow from her little body if he stood beside it, and that it was the same with Minister Noyes; and Sarah Proctor's pale face had flushed up fiercely in assent.

The morning after the little maid Abigail Proctor was buried, Joseph Bayley and his wife Ann came riding down the road from Boston, and they were in brave company, and needed to have but little fear of witches; for the great minister Cotton Mather rode with them, his Excellency the Governor of the colony, two worshipful magistrates, and two other ministers—all on their way to a witch trial in Salem.

And as they neared the Proctor house there was much discourse concerning it and the inmates thereof, many strange and dreadful accounts, and much godly denunciation. And as they reached the curve in the road they came suddenly in sight of a young man and a tall fair maid standing together at the side by some white-flowering bushes. And Sarah Proctor, even with her little sister Abigail dead and her parents in danger of death, was smiling for a second's space in David Carr's face, for the love and hope in tragedy that make God possible, and the selfishness of love that makes life possible, were upon her in spite of herself.

But when she saw the cavalcade approaching, saw the gleam of rich raiment, and heard the tramp and jingling, the smile faded straightway from her face, and she stood behind David in the white alder bushes. And David stood before her, and gazed with a stern and defiant scowl at the gentry as they passed by. And the great Cotton Mather gazed back at that beautiful white face rising like another flower out of the bushes, and he speculated with himself if it were the face of a witch.

But Goodwife Ann Bayley thought only on the little maid at the door. And when they came to the Proctor house she leaned eagerly from the pillion, and she smiled and kissed her hand.

" Why do you thus, Ann ?" her husband asked, looking about at her.

" See you not the little maid in the door ?" she whispered low, for fear of the goodly company. " I trow she looks better than she did. The roses are in her cheeks, and they have combed her yellow hair, and put a clean white gown on her. She holds a little doll, too."

"I see nobody," said Joseph Bayley, wonderingly.

"Nay, but she stands there. I never saw aught shine like her hair and her white gown; the sunlight lies full in the door. See! see! she is smiling! I trow all her griefs be well over."

The cavalcade passed the Proctor house, but Goodwife Ann Bayley's sweet face was turned backward until it was out of sight, towards the little maid in the door.

LYDIA HERSEY, OF EAST BRIDGEWATER

LYDIA HERSEY sat out on the porch carding flax. She had taken her work out there that she might not litter the house. It was Saturday afternoon, and she had set every room in fine order for the Sabbath.

Three tall Lombardy poplar-trees stood in a row on the road line, and their long shadows, like the shadows of giant men, fell athwart the gray unpainted house and the broad grassy yard. At the south of the house was a flower bed of pinks and honeysuckles and thyme, and also a vegetable garden. Beyond that were three bee-hives in a row, with little black clouds of bees around them. Lydia carded assiduously, and never looked up. Her long black lashes lay against her pink cheeks, her full lips were half-smiling, as if she were saying some pleasant thing to herself. Lydia wore her black hair in a braided knot at the back of her head; in front she combed it smoothly down over her ears, then looped it up behind them in two clusters of soft curls. Her flowered chintz gown was cut low in the neck, and she wore a string of gold beads around her long white throat.

Lydia sat very erect as she carded ; her shoulders never wavered with the clapping motion of her hands ; she even sat well forward in her chair, and did not come in contact with its straight back.

Lydia Hersey was noted for the majesty of her carriage as well as her beauty, and was talked of as far as Boston. Young men had been known to come from other villages and walk past her house on the chance of seeing her at a window, although they dared not address her, nor do more than halt and stand for a second with their hats raised like school-boys before the parson or the squire, and that might have been accounted poor reward for a long journey. But there were for these New - Englanders no great pictures by old masters and no famous statues, and Lydia Hersey's beautiful living face, set like a jewel for a moment in a window of the gray old Hersey house, served them instead. The young Abington men, the North Bridgewater men, and the Canton men would go home with their love of beauty all aflame, and never forget Lydia's face in the window ; indeed, it would turn towards them like a portrait, whichever way they moved, through their whole lives. Years afterwards, when these admirers were old men and heard some young beauty praised, they would look scornful and say, " You ought to have seen Lydia Hersey, of East Bridgewater."

A bumblebee flew with a loud buzz past Lydia's head, and she started a little. He flew straight into the open window of the keeping - room. " That's a sign of company," she thought, and she thought also complacently how nicely the house was set in order, and she did not care who came.

The doors were all open as well as the windows. She heard the bee buzzing and striking against the ceiling of the keeping-room. Presently she heard another sound that made her drop her cards in her lap and listen intently. It came from down the street, and sounded like an irregular chorus of horns, a medley of harsh, hollow screeches. Lydia frowned. The sounds grew louder ; there were also great shouts of laughter and clamorous voices. Soon a company of young men came in sight ; there were a dozen of them, and they had great conch shells at their mouths, which they blew between their laughter and merry calls.

Lydia stood up. She laid the cards down on the chair, folded the linen cloth which she had spread on the porch floor carefully over the fluffy heap of carded flax, and brushed all the shreds that she could from her gown. Then she walked,

carrying her beautiful head high, down to the
road. There was a sudden hush when the young
men saw her. They took their conch shells from
their lips, and saluted her respectfully. One
young man, who came foremost of the troop, colored high. One of his comrades nudged him,
and he thrust his elbow back angrily in response.
Lydia took no notice of the other young men, she
walked straight up to this one. He stopped, and
all the others halted at his back.

"Where are you going, Freelove?" said she.

"Not far," he returned, evasively.

"Where?" she demanded.

The young man turned towards his companions. "Move on, lads," he said, in an imperious
voice, which he tried to make good-natured, "I'll
be with you in a moment."

His handsome face was burning. The young
men trooped on; there was a subdued chuckle.
Freelove Keith looked Lydia full in the face, and
his blue eyes were as haughty as her black ones.

"We're going down to see Abraham White and
Deborah," said he.

Lydia stared back at him scornfully. "You
are going down there with those loafers to blow
those conch shells under the windows?" said she.

"Squire Perkins's son is one of 'em," returned
Freelove, defiantly.

"The more shame to him!" said Lydia. "And
the more shame to you, Freelove Keith!"

It seemed as if her bright scornful eyes, full on Freelove's face, could see all the weaknesses that he hid from himself behind his own consciousness, but he did not flinch.

"I don't know what you call shame," he said. "'Tis what the young fellows in East Bridgewater have always done when they have not been asked to a wedding."

"Asked to a wedding," repeated Lydia, contemptuously. "A pretty wedding! Deborah Belcher marrying Abraham White, when he's twice as old as she is, and his wife not dead six months. No wonder she asked nobody to the wedding, marrying old Abraham White for his silver teaspoons and tankard, and his wife's silk gowns and satin pelisse!"

"You don't know that she married him for any such thing," protested Freelove, stoutly, although he had started on this very expedition with a gay contempt for Deborah White. She was a very pretty girl, and once, before he had dared address Lydia Hersey, people had coupled his name with hers. He had gone home with her from singing-school, and kissed her once at a husking.

"Stand up for a girl like that if you want to," said Lydia. She had always had a lurking jealousy of Deborah Belcher. Deborah's hair was very fair, and she had a delicate evanescent bloom like a wild rose. Lydia had often wondered if

Deborah were not prettier than she herself, and if men did not love fair hair better than black.

Freelove Keith did not continue the dispute ; he looked uneasily after his comrades, who were nearly out of sight, even at their slow lingering pace. Now and then the note of a conch shell was heard. "I must go," said he. "Good-day, Lydia."

"Do you mean that you are really going with that noisy crew to blow conch shells under Abraham White's windows, Freelove Keith ?"

"Yes, I am going, Lydia Hersey," returned the young man, hotly ; "and if you thought I'd be ordered back by you before them all, like a whipped puppy, you were mightily mistaken."

Lydia stared at him, she was so full of proud amazement that she would say nothing ; this Freelove Keith had often fretted beneath her rule. but never before openly resisted it.

"Go back to your flax-carding, Lydia," said Freelove, in a softer tone. "See, the flax is blowing all over the yard. I shall be up to see you after supper."

Then Lydia found her tongue. "You haven't been asked to come that I know of," said she. "I don't know as I care to keep company with young men that go blowing horns and shouting through the street, and disturbing decent people."

"Then you needn't," retorted Freelove.

He went quickly down the road after his companions. He was dressed like a farmer, in slouching homespun, but there was a certain jaunty grace about him, and a free swing in his gait, which did not accord with his appearance. He had followed the sea for a living, going as mate on a merchantman, and had been home only for a year and a half, since his father's death, managing the farm.

Lydia went back to the house. She stepped as if she bore a crown on her head instead of a tortoise-shell comb, and had a train to her cotton gown. The wind had indeed stirred the linen cloth, and bits of flax were floating about the yard, but she ignored that. She would not so far unbend her dignity as to gather it up, even with nobody but herself for witness. She folded the linen cloth firmly over the remaining flax, and placed her foot in its buckled shoe on it when she sat down. She fell to work with the cards again. The wild clamor of horns, which she had heard break forth when Freelove joined his comrades, died away in the distance.

Lydia sat there steadily carding flax, as if imbued by nature with the single instinct of industry, like a bee out in the garden. Her lips were tight shut, and no longer smiling; her heart was anxious, but she still made her store of linen as unquestioningly as the bee its honey.

In about an hour the troop of young men with the conch shells returned. Lydia heard them at a distance, and long before they reached the house she sat with stiffer majesty, keeping her eyes so closely upon her work that the flax became a silvery blur. However, she need not have taken the trouble, for Freelove Keith swung past with as scornful a lift of his head as she, and never once glanced her way. And, indeed, the young men all passed very decorously and quietly, and only a few dared raise their eyes towards the queenly figure on the porch, and then only for a second. One of them was Abel Perkins, Squire Perkins's son. He was home from college on a vacation, and was quite looked up to by the village youth, as he was the only collegian among them. Abel Perkins was slight and pale, and walked with a nervous strut; but he wore broadcloth and a fine flowered waistcoat, and carried a gold watch. He even gave a hesitating glance back at Lydia on the porch, turning his little face over his shoulder; but she did not see it. She did not look up from her work until long after the company had passed.

A half-hour later the stage went by, with the four horses at a gallop. A fair face overtopped by white plumes looked out of the surging window. Lydia turned her head hastily, and the red in her cheeks deepened. It was the bride, Deborah White, going with her new husband to spend the honeymoon with his relations in Abington. There was a nice little hair trunk strapped on behind the stage. Lydia eyed it contemptuously when Deborah could no longer see her. She thought, "Maybe his first wife's satin pelisse is in there."

A man emerged from the cloud of dust in the wake of the stage. He was old, and wore his white hair in a queue. He had on a green double cloak, although the day was warm, and walked with a stick, to whose height he accommodated himself at every step with a downward motion of his shoulders. He did not seem to need its support.

When he approached the house, Lydia stood up and courtesied low.

"Good-day, Lydia," said he, in a solemn voice.

"Good-day, sir," she returned, with stately deference; and she ushered the minister, Elihu Eaton, into the fore room, and placed the rocking-chair with the feather cushion for him.

The fore room was close and cool, for the windows had been shut all day to keep out the flies. There was a smell of mint and lavender. The great testered bedstead, with its chintz valance and curtains, stood in one corner. There was a high chest of drawers and a splendid carved oak linen chest, which Lydia's grandmother had brought over from England. On one side of the fireplace was a great cupboard with panelled doors, and that was filled with gallipots. Lydia's father had been a doctor.

Lydia sat beside the window, opposite the minister. There was a restrained defiance in the lift of her chin. Now and then she picked a bit of the flax from her gown.

She knew well why the minister had come. Aunt Nabby Keith had warned her. It was ten months since her banns with Freelove had been published, and she held herself aloof, and would not marry him out of sheer wilfulness and coquetry, the neighbors said. Freelove's aunt Nabby had come to see her only the day before, and talked seriously with her.

"You ain't livin' up to your professions," the old woman had said, "and I'm going to speak plain. If you let this year go by and don't marry Freelove according to your banns, you'll have a good deal to answer for."

"Well, I'll ask nobody else to answer for me," Lydia returned.

"The parson says he's coming to reason with you, Lydia Hersey."

"Let him come," said Lydia; and her head tossed up like a rose in a wind.

And now the parson had come. It was some little space before he opened on the subject in hand. In truth, he stood somewhat in awe, although he did not know it, of this beautiful high-spirited young woman. There had been always a brisk feminine rule in his own house. Even now he sweltered under the weight of the green

double cloak which his wife Sarah had hoisted
upon his slender shoulders because she thought
he had taken cold. The waistcoat, which she
had made to suit her own ideas and not his
requirements, bound his back; his neckcloth,
which she had wound with ardor, half choked
him and fretted his chin.

When at length he reasoned with Lydia Hersey on the matter of her non-fulfilment of the
marriage banns, and the report that she was about
to let the lawful year go by and jilt Freelove
Keith, it was with circumspect solemnity. Lydia's cheeks flamed redder and redder, but her
black eyes never left his face.

"Did you meet Freelove Keith with that noisy
crew, who ought to have been at home at work
in the middle of the afternoon, shouting and
blowing conch shells under Mr. Abraham White's
windows?" she demanded.

The minister admitted that he had, and had
remonstrated with them.

"It would make a better text for a discourse
than some others that meddlesome folks set,"
said Lydia, for she had no fear of any one before
another, not even the minister or the squire. She
stood up. The minister Elihu Eaton's sober
peaked face rising out of his great capes, which
shrugged to his ears, looked up at her. "Either,"
said she, in a masterful way, and yet with a re-
membering sweetness, for the minister looked

suddenly very old to her—"either Freelove Keith
has got to do as I say or I have got to do as he
says before we are married, if the banns have been
cried a thousand years."

Then she went out into the keeping-room, and
presently returned with a tray, on which were set
out a decanter of West India Rum, a little silver bowl of loaf-sugar, a tumbler, and a plate of
pound-cake.

When the minister had partaken of these re-
freshments, he offered a prayer and took his leave.
Lydia courtesied when he went out the door, but
her lips were tightly shut again, for Elihu Eaton,
in his appeal to the Lord, had spoken with more
fire concerning her affairs than he had dared use
towards her. "O Lord, make this, Thy hand-
maiden, to keep to the vows which she has spoken,
and let not a froward mind lead her aside into
strange paths," the minister had said, and more,
and Lydia could not expostulate.

She went into the keeping-room and got supper ready. Lydia Hersey had lived alone ever
since her father's death. All the more reason,
people thought, why she should fulfil her marriage contract with Freelove Keith. There was
she, living all alone in a large house, with a comfortable income, and there was Freelove, who
was no longer so necessary at home since his
sister had married and taken her husband there
to live, and who could easily manage his farm and

live in the Hersey house. There was Freelove, whom everybody liked, yet felt a certain anxiety about, because he had been to sea, and might have seen much evil in foreign ports, going too often to the tavern, people said, and neglecting his farm to go on junketings with idle young men, to Abington or Braintree, and once even over to Boston, and to be away all night. It looked no better, people said, because Squire Perkins's son went with him, and he was college-learned. It was generally conceded that Abel was not as reliable, and would not make as smart a man, as the old squire.

Lydia Hersey saw Abel Perkins again that night. After supper she strolled down the road a little way. She was mindful that Freelove had said he was coming, and she wondered if her rebuff would quite drive him away. Before she started she stood hesitating a moment in the doorway. The evening was cool, and she had put a yellow blanket over her head and bare shoulders.

She thought, angrily, that she would not stay at home and watch for Freelove Keith, when he might not come ; but, on the other hand, she did not want to go away and never know if he had called.

Finally she pulled some sprigs of mint from the bank under the keeping-room windows, and she shut the house door, and stuck them carefully under the sill. Then she went on down

the road, and soon she met Abel Perkins. He
stood about, and took off his hat in a way he had
learned in college, and Lydia courtesied gravely.
Abel was considerably younger than she, and she
had always had a certain disdain for him, in spite
of his being the squire's son. Still it was quite
evident that he humbly admired her, and some
deference was due him for that.

So when he asked humbly if he might walk
with her a way, she said yes, and they went on
together. Alder-trees, faintly sweet in a pale
mist of bloom, stood beside the road; there were
distant peals of laughter, tinklings of cow bells,
and a hubbub of nestward birds. Lydia stepped
proudly along beside the little anxiously smiling
squire's son : her beautiful face looked out of her
yellow blanket as if it were a frame of gold.

Abel Perkins kept glancing up at her and
blushing. " If you had told me that you didn't
want me to go to Abraham White's, I wouldn't
have gone, Lydia," he said, after a while.

" I don't approve of any such goings on," Lydia returned, severely.

" I don't know as they are very becoming,"
said Abel Perkins.

They sauntered on slowly. The sunset light
lay in red-gold patches on the dusty road, some
elm-trees ahead swayed in a mystical, rosy, smoke-
like incense. Presently at the right of the road
showed the red walls of Aunt Nabby Keith's

house out of a thicket of purple-topped lilac-bushes. Freelove suddenly appeared in the road. When he saw Lydia he started, then went on with a jauntier swing. He scarcely nodded as he went by. Lydia held her head like a statue.

"Is he huffy?" whispered Abel.

"I don't know and I don't care," replied Lydia, coldly. But in a second she faced about. "I must go home," said she. "It is getting damp."

Abel went obediently at her side. Freelove was still visible in the road ahead. Lydia talked and laughed very loud, but he did not turn his head, although he must have heard. When they reached the Hersey house, Lydia turned promptly into the yard. "Good-night, Abel," she called, loudly. And Abel Perkins responded with rueful sweetness, for he had thought to be asked in, and went on down the road in Freelove's tracks. Lydia watched him out of sight. She knew he would meet Freelove at the village store, if he did not overtake him. She did not go into the house and disturb the mint on the door-sill. She waited a few minutes, then she also went on a little way to the next house, where lived a young woman mate of hers. She went in and stayed until nearly nine o'clock, and the two girls talked over Deborah Belcher's wedding, but not a word did Lydia say about her quarrel with Freelove.

When she went home, she got down on her

knees in the porch, and examined the mint carefully. It was bright moonlight; not a sprig had
been disturbed. Lydia opened the door and
walked in, trampling the mint ruthlessly.

The next day was Sunday, and she went to
meeting dressed in her best gown, with roses
sprinkled over a blue ground, and her Leghorn
bonnet trimmed with a rose-colored ribbon, and
sat fanning herself calmly with a painted fan
when Freelove entered, but he never looked at
her.

The minister preached from Psalm lxxv. 5,
" Lift not up your horn on high; speak *not* with
a stiff neck," and there was much nudging in the
congregation, and uneasiness among the young
men who had saluted Abraham White and his
bride. Freelove sat straight and stiff, but his
face was red. · Lydia smiled behind her fan.

The next morning Sarah Porter, the girl whom
she had visited Saturday evening, came in. She
had heard that Lydia had really jilted her lover.
She and her mother had watched, and knew that
he had not come courting the night before.

" I hear you and Freelove have fallen out,"
said she. Her lips were smiling archly, but her
eyes were hard and curious.

" There's plenty to hear, if folks keep their
ears pricked up," replied Lydia, and she would
say no more.

She smiled scornfully when presently she

watched Sarah Porter's squat figure go out of the yard. "She didn't find out much," she muttered. "She'd give all her old shoes to get Freelove herself, but he wouldn't look at her."

That forenoon Lydia took her flax-carding out on the porch again. Soon, as she sat there, she saw Abel Perkins coming. He hesitated at the gate. He carried a great bunch of white lilacs. Purple lilacs were plenty in East Bridgewater, but white ones grew nowhere except in the squire's yard.

"Ain't you coming in, Abel?" called Lydia, and she smiled her sweet imperious smile at him.

Abel came up the path, extending the great bunch of lilacs like a propitiatory offering to a deity.

"I thought maybe you'd like a bunch of these white lilacs, Lydia," he said.

"Thank you, Abel; they're real handsome, and I'll put them in a pitcher when I go in," replied Lydia, graciously.

This morning she wore a green and white gown, which made her face still more like a rose. Abel stood leaning against a post of the porch, looking at her, then looking quickly away.

"Have you got any errands or anything you want done, Lydia?" he stammered.

Lydia looked at him; a sudden wicked light came into her eyes. There he stood, in his fine waistcoat and broadcloth, with his handsome

knee-buckles and gold chain.   His hands were
long and slim and white, much whiter than hers.

"Why, yes, Abel," said she; "if you really
want something to do, the pease out in my garden need sticking."

Abel Perkins stared aghast a minute; then he
started eagerly.

"You'll have to go up in the pasture and cut
some brush," said Lydia.

The truth was that Freelove Keith had taken
it upon himself to tend Lydia's garden, which
was but a small one, and she thought with spite-
ful delight how, when he came again, if he came
at all, he would find some of the work done,
and wonder.   But it did not fall out as she had
planned, for presently she heard loud voices
out in the garden, and peering around the corner of the porch, she saw Freelove and Abel, each
with a bundle of brush.

Lydia gathered up her work hastily, and fled
into the house.   She went up to the south chamber, and peeped around the curtain.   Both of her
lovers were sticking the pease, Abel awkwardly,
with trembling haste, and Freelove with a sturdy
vehemence that might have suited Cadmus sow-
ing the dragon's teeth.   Just then there was a
sullen quiet, but presently arose another alterca-
tion.   Lydia spied a long rent in the skirt of
Abel's fine coat.   Soon Abel started towards the
house, and she sat down on the floor of the south

chamber and laughed. She heard a faint voice below calling her, but she did not reply, and Abel dared not search for her in the house.

Lydia peered out again, and saw Freelove at work alone in the garden, but he never once glanced up at the house. She saw Sarah Porter's face, and her mother's over her shoulder, at a window of their house across the yard, and she watched jealously lest Freelove should glance that way; but he did not. When the pease were finished, he went out of the yard, looking neither to the right nor left. Lydia went down-stairs cautiously, to be sure Abel Perkins was gone.

However, when he came again, as he did soon, she greeted him kindly, and smiled sweetly by way of indirect condolence when he told how Freelove Keith had driven him from the garden. Lydia spied the rent, which his mother had neatly mended, in his broadcloth coat.

"Why, Abel, you have torn your fine coat," said she.

Abel blushed. "I tore it getting the sticks for the pease. But 'tis of no account," he said; "and I'm willing to tear it again if there is anything else you want done, Lydia."

"Maybe your mother won't be quite so willing to mend it again," said Lydia.

But presently she brought out the churn, and set Abel Perkins, in his fine clothes, churning cream out on the porch. Sarah Porter called

LYDIA HERSEY

her mother out into their front yard to see, and
Freelove Keith went by ; he went often to see his
Aunt Nabby.

Abel churned until the butter came, and it took
full long, and his fine waistcoat was spattered
with cream ; and then she sent him home like a
little boy. Lydia found many another domestic
task for Abel Perkins, and all on the porch. She
set him carding flax, and spinning, and making
candle-wicks. She found errands also for him to
do, and many commands for him to obey. She
sent him to Abington with a couple of feather
pillows for her aunt, and awkwardly enough he
managed them on horseback. She forbade his
going to Boston on a little trip with some of the
village young men, Freelove being of the party.
Abel Perkins never rebelled against her rule, but
there came a time when Lydia herself arose for
him.

One afternoon he sat on the porch spinning at
the wheel, and Lydia had tied one of her blue
aprons around his waist, when she suddenly
spoke.

"Take off that apron now, and stop spinning,
and go home, Abel Perkins," said she.

Abel jumped up, and stared at her.

"I mean what I say," said she. "If you are
not ashamed for yourself, I am ashamed for you,
and I am ashamed for myself more than I am for
you. No man can make a woman like him by

274

doing everything she tells him to; she only despises him for it. You remember it next time. Now you had better go home and learn your Latin books."

"Can't I come again, Lydia?" said Abel. He was quite pale, and tears stood in his eyes.

But Lydia would not speak softly to him. "No," she replied, "you can't. You mustn't come here wasting your time any more. You must study your books. You are not old enough to go courting; get your college books learned through first."

"Can I come then, Lydia?" he inquired, faintly.

"No," said she; "I shall never want anybody coming again. Take off that apron and go home."

And Abel Perkins obeyed. He looked very dejected and youthful going out of the yard. Lydia went into the house and cried.

Abel stayed away for a week; then he came again. Lydia would not have gone to the door had she known who it was plying the knocker. She never heard the knocker but with a hope that it might be Freelove, although he never came now.

When she saw Abel standing there, she frowned.

"Don't look at me so, Lydia," he pleaded. "I couldn't help coming. I can't eat, and I haven't slept any. I'm sick, Lydia. Mother keeps asking me what the matter is."

Indeed Abel looked ill; he was paler than usual, and had a pinched and woe-begone expression that drew his face down, and made it appear thinner.

"Well, you come in," said Lydia. "I'm going to mix you up some medicine, if you're sick. I know a very good one that my father showed me how to make. It'll cure you right up, Abel."

And Lydia made Abel seat himself on the settle in the keeping-room, and went with a cup and spoon to the cupboard in the fore room, where her father's old gallipots were kept. Then she took from this and that, and mixed carefully, and returned to Abel.

"Here, drink this," said she.

Abel held out his hand, but turned his face away.

"'Tis only a little assafœtida that I put in to quiet the nerves that you smell," said she. "'Tis mostly for the liver. My father used to say that the root of all sickness was the liver, and he did not know but it was the root of all evil. If your liver were in good order you would not fret, Abel Perkins. Drink it down."

And Abel drank it down with an effort.

"Now you'd better go home," said she, "and wait till it takes effect. I'll warrant you'll eat some supper to-night."

"I sha'n't, Lydia, if you don't let me come to see you," said Abel, piteously.

"Yes, you will. How long did you go without your supper when that girl in Abington gave you the mitten ? I ain't the first one you've stopped eating for, Abel Perkins, and you not twenty ! You know it's so."

Abel blushed, and looked down foolishly.

Lydia laughed. "If you keep on this way, you'll starve to death before you come of age," said she. "Now you'd better go home and study your books, and leave such matters alone until you get more sense to manage them. I suppose you will when you've got the college books learned through."

Abel arose. Lydia followed him to the door, and her voice was softer as she bade him good-bye. He looked piteously backward at her as he went out of the yard, but still she was not so touched as she had been before.

"That story about his being so crazy over that girl in Abington was true," she said to herself ; and although she was generous enough to feel relieved that her unlucky lover had an elastic as well as susceptible temperament, and was likely to recover from his wounds, still she disliked him the more for it.

It now wanted only a month for the expiration of the year since Lydia and Freelove's banns had been published. Should they not marry before then, they could not legally, unless they were again published.

LYDIA HERSEY

It was a month since Freelove had set foot in
Lydia's house, or indeed spoken to her. He
came, early in the morning sometimes, and cared
for her garden, but they never exchanged a word.
Everybody said that the marriage was broken off.
Lydia kept on as usual. She had some beautiful
linen in the loom, and she wove as if she were
certainly going to be married. Sarah Porter used
to come in and wonder, but she found out nothing from Lydia, who never spoke Freelove's
name.

"She's making more linen," Sarah told her
mother when she got home, and the two women
speculated anxiously. They knew that Freelove
did not go to see Lydia, at all events, for they
and all the neighbors watched.

When the last day of the year since the banns
came, there was no longer doubt in anybody's
mind, nor was there, indeed, in Lydia's. She
stayed in-doors, and wove her linen in a mechani-
cal fashion. She sat before the great loom, and
it was as if she were playing a harmony of sweet
housewifely industry upon it like a very artist,
but the tears rolled down her cheeks, which were
not rosy that morning.

Had she not listened two months for the sound
of the knocker, she would not have heard it
above the great hum of the loom that afternoon;
but hear it she did, and went to answer it, wiping
her eyes.

Freelove Keith stood in the porch, and out at the gate stood his horse, with a pillion behind the saddle.

"Come, Lydia," said Freelove, "I want you to get on the pillion, and ride over to Aunt Nabby's with me."

"I can't," said Lydia, faintly. "I'm all over flax lint from the loom."

"Put on an apron," said Freelove.

Lydia went into the house, and tied an apron around her waist, and came out again. Freelove lifted her on the pillion, and they rode down the street without a word, until they reached the minister Elihu Eaton's house, which was about half way to Aunt Nabby's.

Freelove drew rein. "Now we'll go in and get married, Lydia," said he.

"Oh, Freelove, *I* can't!" gasped Lydia.

"Now or never," said Freelove, sternly.

"I was going to have a wedding, Freelove, and a brocade gown, and cake—"

"Now or never," said Freelove.

He sprang off the saddle and held up his arms. Lydia slipped down into them, and followed him, trembling, her head drooping, into the minister's house.

When they came out, a stout old woman stood waiting for them at the gate.

"I've got married, Aunt Nabby," said Freelove, with a gay laugh.

279

"Well, I should think 'twas time," replied the old woman. She chuckled; her iron-bowed spectacles flashed back the light. "I've got a bed-quilt made for Liddy, and six yarn socks for you, Freelove," she said; "and I'm going home and bake a pound-cake with some plums in it."

Aunt Nabby went scuttling down the road. Freelove and Lydia remounted, and went back at a canter. Freelove pulled a conch shell from his pocket, and blew as lustily as a herald. Folks ran to the windows, and Lydia hid her blushing face against her husband's shoulder.

THE END

www.ingramcontent.com/pod-product-compliance
Lightning Source LLC
Chambersburg PA
CBHW020506270326
41926CB00008B/755